In *The Relief of Imperfection*, Joan throws a life preserver to women drowning in the undertow of trying to perfect themselves (and anything and anybody they touch) at the expense of their health, sanity, relationships and spiritual welfare. Grab it!

Pamela Heim
Founder, Dean of the BGC School of Women's Ministries
Colorado Springs, Colorado

If you are exhausted from trying to do it all and do it just right, *The Relief of Imperfection* is exactly the balm you need to rest your weary soul and frazzled mind. With the kind of empathy that can only come from a true recovering perfectionist, Joan Webb writes like a friend who has been reading your mind, offering to help you lighten up and lead a more laid-back life.

Becky Freeman Johnson
Author, *Help! I'm Turning into My Mother* and the Heartlite Gift Book Series
Highlands Ranch, Colorado
www.yellowroseeditorial.com

This book gave me hope—and a multitude of practical ways to help me rely on God instead of my imperfect self!

Dr. Jane Kise
Author, *LifeKeys* and *SoulTypes*
Minneapolis, Minnesota

The message of *The Relief of Imperfection* is a powerful reminder that it is our imperfection that makes us human. We are imperfect, and to pretend otherwise diminishes the power of our own story of God's grace in our lives. Joan's eye-opening and relevant sharing kept me reading and nodding my head in agreement— and relief. You will be inspired and nurtured as you read *The Relief of Imperfection,* and you'll also want to give a copy to everyone you know.

Kate Larsen, PCC
Life Coach, Speaker and Author, *Progress Not Perfection: Your Journey Matters*
Minneapolis, Minnesota
www.katelarsen.com

You are going to breathe a sigh of relief when you read *The Relief of Imperfection*. Joan's powerful biblical applications, intriguing stories, practical ideas and the helpful Relief Guides will set you free from whatever level of perfectionism you struggle with. Get ready to allow God to give you new insights and fresh joy about living and relaxing in His power.

Kathy Collard Miller
Speaker and Author, *Women of the Bible—The Smart Guide to the Bible*
Indio, California

What a relief to discover I'm not alone in my struggle and doubt! Reading *The Relief of Imperfection* is like having a heart-to-heart talk with a dear friend who is also a wise and gentle friend—nudging you away from despair and toward solutions. And always, like the best of friends, Joan points you toward the real answer and the real relief found only in the presence of the Lord.

Mary Pierce
Humorist and Author, *When Did My Life Become a Game of Twister?*
Eau Claire, Wisconsin
www.laughlady.com

Joan understands what it is like to be trapped in the world of perfectionism. And because she understands her own life story and journey, she is able to effectively guide others to self-assessment, honesty and freedom. If you carry the heavy weight of trying to fulfill all the unreasonable expectations from other people and from yourself, read this book.

Pete Richardson
LifePlan Facilitator and President of Stratefication Inc.
Lafayette, Colorado

With surgical-like verbal precision, Joan Webb takes an accurate measurement of the harm of perfectionism. She gently and honestly offers wise scriptural advice, affirmation and encouragement to those stuck in this confusing cobweb of perfectionism.

Jim Smoke
Speaker, Life Coach and Author, *Growing Through Divorce*
Palm Desert, California

In *The Relief of Imperfection,* Joan applies the extraordinary coaching gifts of insight, wisdom and practical tools to help women break free from the frenetic drive to fix their lives and those of all around them. Engaging with this unique book can launch recovering perfectionists into a renewed sense of intimacy with God—and a fresh sense of balance and joy in living.

Helen Steinkamp
Director of Women's Ministry, Coast Hills Community Church
Aliso Viejo, California

As a recovering perfectionist who relapses regularly, I was challenged and encouraged by Joan's insights, biblical wisdom and personal illustrations. This is a must-read for all of us susceptible to unrealistic expectations.

Sandra D. Wilson, Ph.D.
Seminary Professor and Retired Family Therapist
Author, *Released from Shame and into Abba's Arms*
Scottsdale, Arizona

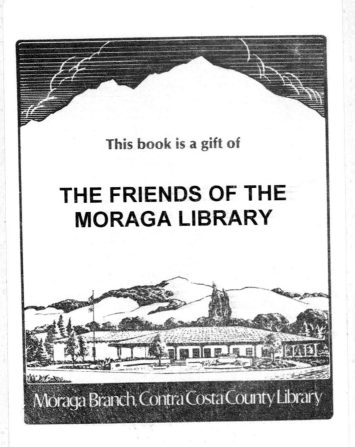

The Relief of Imperfection

For Women Who Try Too Hard
to Make It Just Right

JOAN C. WEBB

Regal

From Gospel Light
Ventura, California, U.S.A.

Published by Regal
From Gospel Light
Ventura, California, U.S.A.
www.regalbooks.com
Printed in the U.S.A.

Some anecdotal illustrations in this book are true to life and are included with the permission of the persons involved. All other illustrations are composites of real situations, and any resemblance to people living or dead is coincidental.

Published in association with the literary agency of WordServe Literary Group, Ltd., 10152 S. Knoll Circle, Highlands Ranch, CO 80130.

Library of Congress Cataloging-in-Publication Data
Webb, Joan C., 1948-
  The relief of imperfection / Joan C. Webb.
    p. cm.
  ISBN 978-0-8307-4481-7 (trade paper)
  1. Perfectionism (Personality trait)—Religious aspects—Christianity. 2. Burn out (Psychology)—Religious aspects—Christianity. 3. Peace of mind—Religious aspects—Christianity. I. Title.
  BV4597.58.P47W43 2007
  248.8'43—dc22
                                                              2007021810

1 2 3 4 5 6 7 8 9 10 / 10 09 08 07

Rights for publishing this book outside the U.S.A. or in non-English languages are administered by Gospel Light Worldwide, an international not-for-profit ministry. For additional information, please visit www.glww.org, email info@glww.org, or write to Gospel Light Worldwide, 1957 Eastman Avenue, Ventura, CA 93003, U.S.A.

I dedicate this book to my husband, Richard.
As you promised, you "stayed with me"
during these focused months of writing The Relief of Imperfection.
Thank you.
Your support, love and respect mean more to me
than you will ever know.
I value our "mutual admiration society"
and love you deeply.

Contents

Preparing for Relief:
What's Wrong with Perfection?

The Relief of
Imperfect Relationships and Families

The Relief of
Imperfect Emotions, Minds and Bodies

The Relief of
Imperfect Life-Work and Service

The Relief of
Imperfect Churches and Culture

The Relief of
Imperfect Dreams, Plans and Decisions

The Relief of
Imperfect Faith, Prayer and Spirituality

The Promise of Relief:
The Smile of Imperfection

Appreciation

Thank you to my literary agent, Greg Johnson, and his wife and partner, author Becky Johnson. I appreciate your wise input, ingeniously humorous ideas and hard work on my behalf. Also, special thanks to editor Kim Bangs and the capable team at Regal Books. Your enthusiastic support is a great encouragement.

I'm grateful for my colleagues and friends in the Intentional Woman Network (www.intentionalwoman.com): Cathy Roberts, Catherine Antone, Kristina Bailey, Lisa Gifford, Gayle Gilbertson, Grayce Gusmano, Holly Hart, Tina Henningson, Teresa Perrine, Joann Pitteloud, Annie Thompson, Audrey Thorkelson, Nicole Guelich and Carol Travilla. I cherish your prayers and encouragement. Carol, thanks for your friendship and invaluable contribution to my life through the years.

How I appreciate my coaching and life plan partners and all the women who shared their powerful stories in this book. I could never fully express how inspired I am by your stories, courage and willingness to share. Thank you to my author friend Mary Pierce for all our telephone JAM (Joan And Mary) sessions and to my writer friend Marsha Crockett for the vital critique and email sessions. And to life coach Kristina Bailey: I treasure our partnership. Thank you to my neighbor and friend Beth Fleming for making sense out of my newspaper and magazine clippings. Gratitude to Kati and Brian Austin and their daughter Bernadette, the caretakers at Strawberry Retreat Center, for making my writing-home-away-from-home so cozy. Thanks to Herb and Beth Rawling for sharing your time-share condo so that I could get away to write. To my friend Sue Theobald: Thanks for coming from Minnesota to Arizona to help me in my office while I wrote—and for your wise feedback as you read and reviewed the chapters. How grateful I am that God brought us together almost 20 years ago. We've seen a lot of imperfect life together.

And to my family: You are the best without a doubt! I love and appreciate you so much. To my generously supportive husband, Richard: My gratitude and love runs deep. It's a joy to dedicate this book to you. To my daughter Lynnette Rasmussen: Thanks for your constant prayers, understanding and wise counsel. To son Rich Webb and son-in-law Adam Rasmussen: Thanks for often asking how I'm doing and for offering support and love. To daughter-in-law Anne Webb: Thanks for organizing the permission forms for the women's stories and verifying the Bible verses and quotes. Thank you to my father, Bob Pressler, and sisters Patty Brock and Karen Boothe for your loving prayers and supportive emails. I also wish to mention my gratitude to my mother-in-law, Mildred Webb, who joined me in praying for this and other projects and left to be with her Lord while I wrote this book. She joins my mother, Dorothy Pressler, in heaven. I miss them both! And special "grandma appreciation" to my adorable grandchildren: Annika, Max, Kirsten, Luke, Lesia and Sam. Your hugs, kisses and smiles inspired me every step of the way.

Foreword

I don't know Joan Webb, but after reading *The Relief of Imperfection*, I know she and I have a lot in common. Like most—dare I say all?—women who seek to serve the Lord and their families, lead productive work lives, maintain healthy friendships, be a vital part of their church and also enjoy their leisure time, Joan has tried to do it all and has failed at times.

It's good to know I'm not the only one. It's even better to know that failing to be perfect isn't the unpardonable sin. That is something we all need to be reminded of—even those of us who write and speak about that very subject.

Just recently, I spoke at a women's retreat. I had packed for springtime in the city, but the retreat was in the mountains where spring had not yet sprung. I ended up having to borrow warm clothes that didn't fit well, including shoes that pinched my toes.

Then, when it came time for me to speak, my brain instantly became muddled with mush. As I kept looking at my carefully planned and color-coded notes, they seemed to be in another language. I thought God had deserted me, which terrified me. I felt that I had failed—failed the women who I thought had expected to hear great things from God through me, and failed God Himself.

Ironically, my topic, "When Perfect Isn't Enough," was about being caught in a performance trap of trying hard to be perfect. The point was that no matter how hard we try, we can't be perfect, but, hallelujah, if we are in Christ, He is perfect for us, in us and through us.

The Bible says that the apostle Paul struggled with an unnamed weakness. Three times he begged God to take it away, but God told him no, that grace was all he needed. God said, "My strength comes into its own in your weakness." Paul went on to say, "Once I heard that, I was glad . . . I quit focusing on the handicap and began appreciating [it as a] gift. . . . Now I take limitations in stride and with good cheer. These limitations that cut me down to size . . . just let Christ take over. And so the weaker I get, the stronger I become" (2 Cor. 12:8-10, THE MESSAGE).

I had wanted to be flawless, but I forgot that I wasn't and couldn't be in and of myself. However, when I thought about it after I had returned home, I ended up being glad that I wasn't flawless. My brain mush, the pinching shoes and the wrong clothes had actually been gifts from God. He had allowed me to be uncomfortably imperfect so that He might be perfect for me, in me and through me.

There is great relief in imperfection, which Joan Webb lays out in this book. As a recovering perfectionist, Joan knows the anxiety that haunts those of us who try to be that which we aren't and never will be: perfect. Only God is perfect, and as hard as we might try, we will never attain or achieve perfection. But, as Joan reminds us, that's good news.

"The truth is," she writes, "all of us regular people are human and flawed. We need a Savior. And there's good news: We have one." Not only do we have a Savior who saves us from the punishment and penalty of our sins, but He also gives us His perfection and invites us to rest in that.

"Are you tired? Worn out? Burned out on religion?" Jesus asks in Matthew 11. "Come to me. Get away with me and you'll recover your life. I'll show you how to take a real rest. Walk with me and work with me—watch how I do it. Learn the unforced rhythms of grace. I won't lay anything heavy or ill-fitting on you. Keep company with me and you'll learn to live freely and lightly" (vv. 28-30, *THE MESSAGE*).

Did you read that? Nowhere does the Scripture say to knock yourself out to be perfect. Rather, it states we should walk with Jesus—to let Him be the perfect one, and rest in that. Ironically, as we do so, we end up doing greater things for His kingdom because they're His things in the first place. That's what Joan reminds all of us who struggle with perfection and battle the tyranny of bigger, better, faster and more—those of us who over-achieve, overwork, under-rest and under-enjoy life.

The Relief of Imperfection is just that—relief. "Imagine," Joan writes, "relief, joy, and peace coexisting with imperfection."

I do believe that Joan's message will help a lot of women to breathe, and that's quite important, I hear. Just read the title— *The Relief of Imperfection*. Doesn't it cause your shoulders to relax? Wait until you read the rest of this book. You might just get up and dance.

Nancy Kennedy
Recovering Perfectionist and Author, *When Perfect Isn't Enough*
Crystal River, Florida
www.nancykennedybooks.com

Read This First!

A Letter to My Reader-Friend

Dear Reader-Friend,

I wish we could sit together and chat over a cup of vanilla-flavored chai tea (if you would rather have a coffee or cappuccino, that's fine with me. I promise not to push my favorite hot drink on you!). I don't know what brought this book into your hands, but I'm glad you found it. What I do know is that over the years as I've mentioned the word "perfectionism" in workshops, seminars, coaching, life planning and Intentional Woman groups, people—both women and men—take a few steps back. It seems that none of us wants to be associated with *that* word and its connotations. But I think there is an incredible amount of misunderstanding and misinformation about perfectionism and its related systems.

Recently I chatted with a talented young woman who acknowledged that, like me, she struggles with the trying-too-hard-to-make-it-just-right philosophy—but she wouldn't admit the *P*-word. "I really don't think I'm a perfectionist," she said. "After all, I certainly don't look like one."

I frequently hear similar statements as I interact with friends, associates, and coaching and life-plan clients, and talk with women across the nation or even in other countries. I remember the single executive woman climbing the corporate ladder, the harried mother of toddlers, the isolated pastor's wife, the creative grade-school teacher, the overworked nurse, the woman longing for a husband, the confused college student, the caring Bible teacher, and that grandmother concerned about her grand-children. Each had her own unique situation, but all struggled to make everything just right.

Perfectionism wears many faces, includes all personality styles and cuts across cultural lines. It doesn't always line up canned goods in alphabetical order on the kitchen shelf, wash a car in freezing weather, shine shoes when they don't need it, refuse to leave the house if one hair is out of place, or insist that a report be edited endlessly. Perfectionism is more subtle than that. It has to do with unreasonable expectations—how we belittle ourselves and others for having human (we translate that word as "weak") thoughts and emotions, inconsistent faith or less-than-excellent plans, accomplishments, families, bodies or dreams.

The problem is that when we try too hard to make it just right, eventually we get bone tired—and then we become candidates for physical, mental, emotional, social and/or spiritual burnout. Perfectionism and increased anxiety are kissing cousins. When in active mode, the cousins tend to alienate others with their overworking, overdoing, over-caring, over-giving and trying-too-hard behavior. It's ironic. In the push to have and be *the best,* we often fail to enjoy life, God and others.

The Relief of Imperfection is for women who try to do everything, anything or at least *something* perfectly in order to make sure their lives turn out the way they *should.* It's for the many caring women (me included) who believe—at least at some level—that it is possible to accomplish textbook-perfect emotional responses if we just do life *right.* This book offers hopeful relief for those of us who attempt to be more than excellent in our marriages, parenting, careers, friendships, church or community involvements *and* spirituality.

Yet perhaps you've detected that these rigidly exacting habits, goals, ideas and expectations are actually self-defeating. I have. The women I interact with long to know that they can lead less demanding lives and still be valuable people—that it will be okay with God if they decide to slow down, relax and smile amidst their imperfect realities.

When I talked with my literary agent, Greg Johnson, and his writing consultant wife, Becky, about my next writing project, they asked for the main theme. I said, "Encouragement for those who try too hard to make it all just right."

"Hmm. That's too long," responded Greg.

"I agree," I said. "Yet that's the essence of my message."

"Sounds like the joy of imperfection," remarked Becky.

"That's it!" I screamed inside. (I practiced more decorum when responding aloud.) After corresponding back and forth, the relief of imperfection theme rose to the top. Becky says there's something about it that causes her shoulders to relax. Mine, too. My prayer for you, Reader-Friend, is that you will also experience this relief and relaxation.

Perhaps you would like to ask a friend, colleague, church group or neighborhood group to join you in reading this book and working through the coordinating Relief Guides, which correspond to each of the eight sections of the book. You can certainly read *The Relief of Imperfection* and complete the Relief Guides on your own, but I encourage you to share your insights with a friend or colleague. This goes for extroverts *and* introverts! *Impression without expression can lead to depression, or at least intense frustration.*

You might meet for breakfast or during lunch hour to share your responses and inspiration. Or you could start a women's group at church, with your neighbors, or with the mothers of your child's classmates. If it's impossible to meet face to face, consider doing the exercises on your own and then connecting by telephone or email. You could use the book in an eight-week study for your Sunday School class or women's Bible study. Or you and your friends might do the eight sections during a weekend get-away.

I suggest you start a "Relief Journal" to record your discoveries and responses. (It might be a fancy journal, a three ring binder, a steno pad or notebook paper bound with a rubber band or ribbon. It doesn't matter!) Remember, the Relief Guides are for your benefit, so you always have options about when, where, how and whether to complete them. In life coaching, the response to a next step, assignment, idea or plan always includes options. It is up to you how you follow up. You may respond with:

1. *Yes:* "I'll answer these questions and do the exercises after reading the chapters."
2. *No:* "Doesn't work for me right now."
3. *Renegotiation:* "I don't have the opportunity or time this week, but I will next week" or "I'll answer some, but not all."
4. *Later:* "I'll think about it and decide by _____ [date/time]."

If you're doing the Relief Guides in a group setting and would like additional questions, ideas or exercises, visit www.reliefofimperfection.com and access the Facilitator Tips or Group Discussion drop-down menu. Above all, have fun doing the Relief Guides—laugh, reflect and learn. As you do, I believe you will:

1. Become more aware of pesky perfectionistic thinking in specific areas of your life, even though you may not consider yourself a true perfectionist.

2. Gain a new perspective on what Scripture teaches about accepting your human limitations and imperfections.

3. Recognize misconceptions that threaten the fulfillment of your God-given goals, hinder intimacy in

your relationships and alienate you from the God
you seek to know and serve.

4. Continue to pursue excellence, yet escape self-
    defeating perfectionism.

5. Relax and realize that everything doesn't need to be
    so difficult and that some things can actually be easy,
    fun and smile-able.

What a relief! Please join me on this continuing adventure
of learning to celebrate life—imperfect though it may be.

Breathing deeply,
Joan

Preparing for Relief:
What's Wrong with Perfection?

I Was Perfect Once, but I Didn't Like It Much

It is a wonderful thing to be alive!
Ecclesiastes 11:7, *TLB*

"I'm going now," said my administrative assistant. "Thank you for everything."

"All the best to you in your new career," I said. As she walked out the door, she handed me an envelope. When back in my office, I opened it. Inside her bon voyage card she had hand-written this message: "Joan, I hope someday you can stop and smell the roses."

I glanced around to make certain no one was leaning over my shoulder reading the note. Her message embarrassed me, because it reminded me that my zealous attempts to hide my perfectionism-induced exhaustion were unsuccessful. Still, I couldn't help chuckling. Bonnie correctly assessed my unrealistic mindset and suggested that I slow down, stop trying so hard to make it all just right and start enjoying life. The writer of Ecclesiastes would have made the same recommendation: "Better one handful with tranquility than two handfuls with toil and chasing after the wind" (4:6).

Several years have passed since the day I read that stop-and-sniff-the-roses message, and I've made some positive intentional adjustments in my attitudes, beliefs, lifework and personal roles. I've learned to relax and celebrate life—imperfect though it may be (at least much of the time). Yet recently I've noticed that I'm being sucked back into the trying-too-hard-to-make-it-just-right syndrome. I'm bombarded with messages that imply I'm still not doing life quite right.

Over-the-Top Expectations

A tremendous amount of the information out there comes down to two statements: One of these is "You're deficient." And the other is "If you buy this, it will fix that."

MIKE DASH, HIGH-TECH INDUSTRY CONSULTANT [1]

Books, magazine and newspaper articles, reality and news shows, commercials, Internet pop-ups, websites, stores, doctors, schools, fitness centers and even churches present methods and habits we can and should adopt to look younger and trimmer; be healthier and more energetic; work faster and better at home or in the office; be more successful; make extra money; maintain consistently satisfying relationships; obtain more education; improve our cooking, time management, home décor, parenting and grand-parenting skills; build a bigger, better and more organized house; be a more loving mate; enjoy increased fun and additional exciting vacations; and enhance social interaction with neighbors and colleagues—all while keeping up with technology, avoiding overload, reducing anxiety and stress, developing personally and spiritually, giving generously to the hungry and hurting, and doing all with greater love, patience, joy, self-control, peace, persistence, passion and care. (I don't know about you, but just rereading that sentence makes me want to lie down and take a long nap—perhaps for several days!)

Jerry White, author of *Making Peace with Reality*, says it this way: "We live in a different world—one that is accelerating with change and fraught with uncertainty. We cannot alter its march. It is our reality."[2] We live in an unreasonably demanding age of over-choice, over-knowledge, over-tech, overexposure, over-responsibility and overachievement. Too many tasks to complete, roles to perform, challenges to accept, activities and events to plan and attend, hurting people to help, bills to pay, options to consider, books to read; too much information to assimilate, new technology to learn, tragedy and heartache on the screen, news and media bombarding the airwaves, blurring of reasonable boundaries and—*sigh!*—too little respite and renewal.

"Overburdened, overworked, and overwhelmed. What started as a joy became drudgery, and I felt like giving up. Nothing is harder to bear than a burden we're not called to carry . . . And while there are many needs, God has not asked us to meet every one."

Joanna Weaver, *Having a Mary Heart in a Martha World*[3]

From my own experience and from working with coaching clients, business and ministry associates, as well as talking with women in the audiences of our Intentional Woman seminars and workshops, I've noticed something: This saturated and accomplishment-oriented lifestyle often leads to an exaggerated sense of power and entitlement.

Sometimes it's blatant (as in the ostentatious lifestyles and work ethics of those recently convicted with cheating and manipulating their way to influence and control), but more often this inflated sense of power comes on subtly. If you're reading this book, you likely long to serve God *and* grow to be the woman He created you to be. In addition, you probably want to accomplish this in the manner the Bible teaches: with excellence, joy, love, peace, self-control, goodness and patience (see Gal. 5:22).

Like many other women with a heart for God, you're probably not purposefully or aggressively seeking dominance or control. However, as Donald McCullough states in *The Consolations of Imperfection*, "No one except God can carry the weight of everyone's safety and health and happiness and fulfillment in life. To guarantee this for even one person will soon have anxiety tearing you apart like a lion enjoying a fine meal."[4]

The Subtle Allure of Power

Great is the Lord and most worthy of praise; his greatness no one can fathom . . . his understanding has no limit.
PSALMS 145:3; 147:5

"Judy has boundless energy and limitless creativity. I can always count on her to be available when needed," said my friend Judy's boss during an awards meeting. "She's our company's greatest asset. We simply couldn't function without her."

These comments are high praise coming from an employer. Or are they? Take a second look at the descriptions used to commend Judy: boundless energy, powerless without her, limitless creativity, always available. These phrases describe only one: God.

Some of us slide into a position that breeds this exaggerated sense of power, as Judy did. Talented, high-achieving, goal-oriented people like my friend are usually conscientious, dedicated, reliable and loyal. Sometimes they cross over the line of reason and try too hard to make it just right. Others, like Judy's boss, notice and often nudge the unrealistic process along by requesting or expecting more than is humanly possible. Consider the following story from Becky Lee, a personal life coach and former corporate executive:

> Feeling rushed, exhausted, agitated and overwhelmed, I boarded a plane headed for London just as they closed the door and started to taxi down the runway. I located my seat next to the window and climbed clumsily over a woman with extremely long legs. Once buckled in, I sighed with relief that there was an empty seat between us.
>
> I pulled out the hard copy of the presentation I was to give as soon as we landed at Gatwick International. I reviewed my talk and munched on the granola bar I found at the bottom of my purse. After rechecking my papers and eating my breakfast or lunch (it could have been either—I couldn't remember the last time I ate), I headed to the lavatory to express enough milk to send home to Ohio so that my husband could feed our baby daughter. I planned to send it by overnight air before I went into the meeting.
>
> Once inside the tiny toilet, I shook my head as if to wake up from this nightmare. "What are you doing, Becky?" I whispered. "This is ridiculous. Who do you think you are? God?" Talk about an exaggerated sense of power! Pushed beyond reasonable limits, I saw the truth: I was sliding down the slippery slope to burnout. I decided right there to stop the madness. When I arrived home after that whirlwind trip, I told my husband I would never do that again. For way too long, I had tried too hard to make it all work. I knew the solution for me was to resign my lucrative position. I did, and I never looked back.

Perfection's Quandary

As you read Becky's and Judy's stories, perhaps you thought or even said, "That's not me. I would never allow myself to be in a position like that." Or maybe you thought these two women were reading your personal journal! Certainly not every woman exhibits her unrealistic expectations with the same approach. Perhaps this entire concept seems a little fuzzy to you right now. If so, I encourage you to keep reading. Within these pages, many other women will share their trying-too-hard-to-make-it-just-right stories. Awareness, discovery, connection *and* relief are on the way!

After facilitating a workshop on *The Relief of Imperfection* one morning, I went to a nearby restaurant with several participants. Halfway through my chicken salad, the woman sitting beside me said, "But I always thought perfection was *good*—and that perfectionism was even better!" I've since discovered others are equally confused. Although there are some who avoid the *P*-word like a plague, some wear it proudly like a Girl Scout sash across their chests. After all, what's wrong with perfection?

The dictionary defines the word "perfection" as "the state of being complete in every way; without defect; flawless; completely accurate; pure, most excellent or faultless."[5] Obviously, nothing is wrong with perfection; it defines the nature and character of God. He is perfect in every possible way in each circumstance on any day of any century. The quandary with perfection surfaces when we as God's created human beings attempt to make our own situations, family members, jobs, homes and emotions flawless, sinless or perfect. It isn't possible.

Have you experienced the following? You try, teach, plan, think, research, study, organize, affirm, strive, maneuver, deny, avoid, control and still come up (for air) empty-hearted? I'm not proud of it, but I admit I have. Here's a sample of a former silent yet fervent prayer: "Dear Lord, I pray that all limitations, weaknesses, defects, pain, hurt, mistakes, embarrassment and imperfection in my personal and public life, relationships and circumstances be eliminated." A little exaggerated? Maybe, but not much. The results of this petition? Ongoing disappointment that I believed I had to hide in order to appear godly. As Dr. Larry Crabb writes in his book *Inside Out*, "The simple fact we must face is this: Something is wrong with everything. No matter how closely we walk with the Lord, we cannot escape the impact of a disappointing . . . world."[6]

Entitled to What?

That your faith might not rest on men's wisdom, but on God's power.
1 CORINTHIANS 2:5

Striving for what remains impossible is a sure path to frustration. It can lead to disillusionment, anxiety, dissatisfying relationships, pretending, isolation and loss of the intimacy and love we seek. *Perfectionism*, the dictionary indicates, is "the theory that moral, religious, or social perfection can be attained by mortals."[7] Some of us live as if we believe this theory. This underlying premise can give us an inflated sensation of control and privilege that edges out God, faith and even reality.

Although human beings can share in God's energy and creativity, helpfulness and power, we do not possess these qualities in infinite measure. To believe we do is a recipe for physical, mental and spiritual exhaustion. To think we're *entitled*—as intentional women with hearts for God—to the most superb devotional lives, Bible studies, families, husbands, children, relationships, churches, work lives and residences is a set-up for disappointment and frustration.

This concept recently hit home (literally) for Lynnette, a caring young professional woman who now stays home to raise her three little girls:

For years I worked diligently to free myself from the tyranny of unrealistic expectations. Yet recently I became upset and confused like I'd been before. Having two more children made our existing home cramped for a family of five, so we decided to build a new house. We researched, prayed and genuinely believed we made the right move.

I started planning how I'd decorate, and excitedly chose beautiful upgrades. But shortly after signing our contract, I began to doubt. I liked the house, but felt dissatisfied with the lot. I thought I'd miss the park across the street from our current home. I worried about the power lines one-quarter of a mile away and the smaller backyard. *Will the girls' toys fit in the yard? Will the power lines obscure my early morning view?*

If we opted out, we'd lose our earnest money. Still, I schemed to fix the problem. I researched other lots as they opened up. Reviewing the development plans, I saw four lots with larger backyards. I fixated on the one with the biggest backyard located directly on a park. *That will make me happy. I'll have my dream house and never move again.*

Preoccupied with disappointment, I studied the backyard view of every house I passed. When jealousy welled up, I wanted it to go away. I memorized Hebrews 13:5: "Let your conduct be free from covetousness. But be content with such things as you have. For He Himself has said, 'Never will I leave you nor forsake you.'" *Father, this is coming between us. I don't want that. Please help me.*

My internal scheming (I even researched dropping the contract and going with another builder in a different community) affected our marriage, too. Adam tried to understand, but it was difficult for him because he felt excited and happy that he could provide this new home for us. After praying, struggling and journaling for days, I finally saw how I had begun to feel *entitled* to one of the neighborhood's few premium lots. I let my concerns turn to worry until they became completely overblown.

I can't even see the power lines from the backyard, and we'll live right across the street from a greenbelt. Our backyard is big enough for the swing set my husband built and the floor plan fits our entertaining and ministry values.

Although not an easy process, I realize that I had allowed the trying-too-hard-to-make-it-just-right mindset to consume me again. I experienced the frown of perfectionism and did *not* like it. It felt heavy, preoccupying, energy-draining and divisive. It pushed me away from my true desire to glorify God and enjoy His presence.

My real home is being prepared in heaven. That home will be perfect. For now I'm satisfied and happy to live here with my family and the liberating smile of imperfection.

Perfectionism? Not Me!

Now we see things imperfectly as in a poor mirror,
but then we will see everything with perfect clarity.
All that I know now is partial and incomplete, but then I will know
everything completely, just as God knows me now.
1 CORINTHIANS 13:12, NLT

"Your daughter Joan will most certainly have a nervous breakdown before her eighteenth birthday if she keeps this up," said my third-grade teacher.

"I don't think so," replied my mother during the annual parent-teacher conference. "She's just eight years old, after all." They completed their time together without Mother showing her displeasure with Mrs. Harris's (not her real name) assertion. Yet when Mom shared the story with me later, I could tell that she felt annoyed at my teacher and convinced that I—her first-born child—would *never* allow the prediction to come true.

Even in those early elementary years, I did not enjoy acknowledging limitations. I wanted to read every book available to me and be the student with the most book reports. I could not fathom seeing a red mark on my worksheets. I can remember wanting to be more than a top student—I also wanted to love and serve God with all my heart. I longed to do everything possible to make certain God was pleased with me. During the years when many little girls are thinking about hopscotch and popsicles, I was serious about my intellectual and spiritual growth. If they'd had Day Planners back then, I probably would have added a red one to my Christmas list!

In case you're wondering, my teacher was wrong, and Mother was right. I did not have a nervous breakdown at 18 years of age. I waited until I was almost 40! (Technically speaking, it was "severe burnout." More about this later.)

"Personal integrity, it seems to me, calls for owning the whole of one's experience—the painful as well as the joyous, the shameful as well as the praiseworthy, the shadows as well as the light, the limitations as well as the possibilities."

Donald McDullough, *The Consolations of Imperfection*[8]

I've always attempted to plan well, cover all the bases and operate in every one of my roles by working hard and avoiding mistakes. I really don't enjoy seeing my flaws—or anyone else's. It's embarrassing to admit that I worked too hard to make it all just right, but I guess that's my truth. If I'm not careful, I push my desire to be Christlike into God's solo territory of perfection. And each time I acknowledge that it's happening again, I don't like it much.

Trying and Working Too Hard

In her book, *Working Ourselves to Death*, Diane Fassel contends that although workaholics often work a great deal, they aren't *always* working. Some avoid work, some work in compulsive spurts, and others procrastinate. All have a latent perfectionist streak. Fassel defines workaholics this way:

> "Work addict" is a broad term that covers rushaholics, careaholics, busyaholics—any person who is driven to do too much, whether that person works sixty hours a week or runs around like a chicken with its head cut off. In its narrowest sense, workaholism is an addiction to action; but the action takes many forms. . . . Some work addicts appear motionless, but their minds are racing. The type of action may vary, but the process is the same: You leave yourself.[9]

Of course, the most noticeable workaholic in our culture is the "obsessive worker." She works long hours, taking on project after project, often feeling misunderstood and underappreciated for the significant contributions she makes. Yet she feels compelled to keep doing; it is a matter of identity for her. If she stopped to rest, it would prove she is inferior, lazy or both—and that would be unthinkable.

A "binger" works in spurts, but with great intensity. Work, projects, tasks and accomplishments become the medication of choice so that she doesn't have to feel her emotions, deal with her disappointments or ask deep questions.

Then there is the "work anorexic." She's afraid she'll do it wrong, so she procrastinates, and the resulting guilt immobilizes her.

Each workaholic is disturbed by her humanness, because human beings need consistent sleep, nutritious food, interaction with others, respite and relaxation. In addition, as a human being she makes mistakes and has needs, emotions and disappointments—and that exasperates her. To stave off the unpleasantness that's inherent in these human experiences, she keeps working and trying hard to make it all better.

In the zealous pursuit of excellence, schools and universities produce children and young people obsessed with flawless performance in athletics, academics and extracurricular activities. Pressured by church and family, homemakers may become overly focused on trying too hard to make it all just right in the interest of being picture-perfect wives, mothers, daughters and neighbors. As Robin Lindberg, a caregiver, wife and mother of two boys, writes:

> *Over-care!* When I heard that characteristic of perfectionism and overload, I knew it described my life.
>
> Several months ago, my husband, Doug, and I moved into a new house. Of course, our two sons (8 and 10 years old) moved in, too. Doug's 97-year-old grandmother, Gammie, also lives with us. I have been her full-time caregiver for over a year now, and we hope she stays with us for the rest of her life. We all love our new place—it has four bedrooms and a large room and laundry area in the basement.

In addition to Doug, our sons, Gammie and me, my sister-in-law Lauren is living here too, while maneuvering through a traumatic divorce. Her 20-year-old daughter, Margo, moved in also, and her 17-year-old daughter, Nickee, spends several nights a week as well.

When our good friends Walter and Eve divorced and sold their house, we offered Eve a place to live for a while until she gets back on her feet. At the beginning of the year, my friend Julie went back to work, so I became the full-time babysitter for her precious 3-year-old son, Morgan. This week, we have another family with two young sons coming to visit.

We have a house full! Most of the time, it feels great—I'm grateful for a husband who enjoys helping people just as I do and thankful to be a stay-at-home mom in a new house with more space. I pray that my service gives witness and honor to Jesus so that the members of my family and my guests might come to know God in a personal way.

But my *over*-caring shows up when I try to fix everything for everyone. I want to take away everyone's pain. It is as if I want to be their savior. Recently I realized that when I try too hard to make it all just right, I'm really attempting to play God. It wears me out and sends me into overload. At the same time, it robs those I love from learning the lessons God wants to teach them. I might even stand in the way of them coming to know Him personally. That thought makes me sad.

I understand what perfectionistic-overload means for me: It's when I try to go beyond my human limitations and do what only God and the other person can do together. It is then that I experience exhaustion and self-doubt. Changing the way I relate to the people around me puts me squarely into unfamiliar and un-comfortable territory. For now, I'm content to be in the process of adjusting my unrealistic expectations, trusting God for what I can't do and experiencing sur-prising spurts of joy in the midst of my sometimes overwhelming circumstances.

Coexisting with Imperfection

Perfectionism is the belief that it's possible for everything to be exactly as we think it should, and that this would make us totally, blissfully happy.
VERONICA RAY, *I'M GOOD ENOUGH*[10]

Over-care, overwork and the trying-too-hard-to-make-it-just-right syndrome often surface when we confuse who we are as God's unique and valuable creation with what we can or cannot *do*. Yet if you and I had everything just the way we wanted, it would not be perfect. Our dreams, thoughts, desires and goals are laced with flaws.

Perfection on this earth is not possible. At first glance, this state-ment may seem discouragingly negative. Yet I remember how this truth gradually seeped into my mind and eventually satu-rated my heart. My shoulders started to relax and I gained per-mission to breathe more deeply. Even now as I write this, I can't help smiling. I feel relieved. Imagine relief, joy and peace co-existing with imperfection.

One day, everything and everyone who trusts in God will be faultless. Although it may not be how we envision a perfect eternity, it will be the way God wants it. And we'll delight in it. We'll worship the triune God with perfect pitch, complete ado-ration and unimpaired service. It will happen. Letting go of our need to do and make it all just right *now* releases us to hope in the glorious future God has planned for us later. As Paul writes:

> All creation anticipates the day when it will join God's children in glorious freedom from death and decay . . . And even we Christians, although we have the Holy Spirit within us as a foretaste of future glory, also groan to be released from pain and suffering. We, too, wait anxiously for that day when God will give us our full rights as his children, including the new bodies he has promised us (Rom. 8:21-23, *NLT*).

God offers you and me an ongoing *yes* to life—not a one-time solution to the trying-too-hard dilemma, but a continuing process of spiritual enrichment. He encourages us to live in the midst of our less-than-perfect reality with Jesus as our companion, teacher, soul mate, savior and friend. In every life role, Jesus invites us to live *freely* and *lightly*, even though we dwell in a relentless age of over-the-top expectations:

> Are you tired? Worn out? Burned out on religion? Come to me. Get away with me and you'll recover your life. I'll show you how to take a real rest. Walk with me and work with me—watch how I do it. Learn the unforced rhythms of grace. I won't lay anything heavy or ill-fitting on you. Keep company with me and you'll learn to live freely and lightly (Matt. 11:28-29, *THE MESSAGE*).

I invite you to join me on this adventure, a journey to freedom. It will take commitment, because this new way of thinking and behaving is not familiar to us who have long practiced this trying-too-hard-to-make-it-just-right philosophy. However, the truth is that only God is absolutely perfect, and He promises to help, guide, teach and give us courage. We can change. We can grow. We can heal.

Isn't that a relief?

Lord, I know sometimes I try too hard to make it all just right
and this contributes to my anxiety and disillusionment levels.
I know I can't be perfect, but sometimes I think I should be.
Then I try even harder. I'm really tired of living this way.
So I'm coming to You just as You asked me to do.
I want to live "freely and lightly" with You as my coach.
Teach me the "unforced rhythms of Your grace."
I'm listening.

CHAPTER 2

Doesn't God Want Me to Be Perfect?

God has our pictures in his wallet. He loves us. He wants us to love ourselves and each other.

Kathy Vick, *Lessons in Buoyancy: Letting Go of the Perfect Proverbs 31 Woman*[1]

THUD! Every man, woman and child in the hotel lobby froze and stared at me as I fell back toward the sidewalk. The *thud* was my head banging against the glass door. The manager hurried to my side.

"That was dumb," I murmured.

"You okay?" he asked.

"Well, I guess I thought it was an open door," I answered feebly. I remembered walking confidently toward the table displaying complimentary morning papers. All I wanted was to read the current news. Instead, I walked forcefully into a recently cleaned picture window.

"That was loud!" said the manager. "Your forehead's all red, but I don't see any blood. Glad your sunglasses didn't cut you. Think you're going to be alright?"

"I'll be fine, thanks," I responded as I walked away, blurry-eyed.

What was that, Joan? That's never happened before. How could you have done that? Then remarkably, my thoughts shifted. *Hey, it was a mistake!* And just as quickly shifted again. *Yeah sure, J.C. Not only was it a mistake, but a very public example of imperfection. Wonder if they all think you're tipsy this early in the day.*

I couldn't stifle an internal chuckle. Nor could I wipe the spontaneous grin from my face. Imperfection happens. It just does.

No Perfect Saints!

With all its imperfections, ragged endings, and surprises,
real life is alive with possibility.

<small>ENID HOWARTH AND JAN TRAS, *THE JOY OF IMPERFECTION*[2]</small>

I was at the hotel to work on *The Relief of Imperfection* manuscript and needed a break. Just before walking into the floor-to-ceiling glass window, I surprised myself by writing the following words in my journal:

> You know what? I don't think there is a single biblical character (spiritual giant or not) who was consistently pure, good or wise. Not one!
>
> Abram lied about his relationship with wife Sarai (Gen. 12:10-20). Twice. David committed adultery and killed to cover his tracks (2 Sam. 11:3-7). Jacob deceived his father and played favorites with his sons (Gen. 37:2-3). Sarah shamed and ridiculed her employee Hagar (Gen. 16:6). Paul and John Mark had a public ministry split (Acts 15:36-40). Peter impetuously cut off a soldier's ear in defense of His friend Jesus and then denied even knowing Him (John 18:10,26). James and John jockeyed for higher status, disregarding the others on Jesus' team (Mark 10:35-41). Each had unique flaws, limitations, imperfect relationships, quirky habits or faulty reasoning. Some even broke the law. It seems like the highest-profile leaders made the poorest choices and biggest blunders.

Yet God proclaimed Abraham a faithful friend (Jas. 2:23) and David a man close to his heart (Acts 13:22). Jacob experienced God face to face (Gen. 23:30) and Sarah received her deepest desire—a miracle pregnancy (Gen. 24:36). God blessed both the ministries of Paul and John Mark (Acts 15:39-41; 2 Tim. 4:11), built His entire New Testament Church on Peter's leadership (Matt. 16:18) and kept brothers James and John on His executive staff (Matt. 17:1-3).

God's Expectations

There's not one totally good person on earth,
not one who is truly pure and sinless.
ECCLESIASTES 7:20, *THE MESSAGE*

Over the years, I've studied and read about these and other biblical folks. I examined their experiences, choices and faith, receiving spiritual encouragement and direction from their stories. But perhaps I've never honestly examined the cumulative picture. Now I'm astounded by what I discovered: not one totally godly human role model in the entire Bible. (Well, except Jesus—who was 100-percent God and 100-percent man.)

So what *are* God's expectations? Didn't He want Abraham, David, Jacob, Sarah, Paul, John Mark, Peter, James and John to be perfect? Doesn't He want you and me to be perfect? Yes—and no. Yes, because His divine standards are absolute and unspoiled. No, because we are not God-clones. He doesn't expect us to do the impossible and be flawless.

Yes!

Yes, God wants (and *needs*) us to be perfectly good in thought and deed in order for us to have unrestricted communication together. He is all knowing, all powerful, all good, all right, all just and capable of seeing everyone and everywhere at the same time. I am not—and although I don't wish to step on your toes, neither are you. It is contrary to His perfect nature to be intimate with sin or wrong (yours and mine included)—not because He tries to be difficult, judgmental or stern, but because He is *God*.

There is a gap between who God is and who you and I are. He cannot say, "Well, I realize you're inherently flawed and disbelieving, but it doesn't matter. I'll just pretend you're perfect and ignore that you are often self-preoccupied, untruthful, controlling and emotionally abusive to those you've promised to love." If He did that, He would be untrue to Himself—and then He would not be *God*.

Personally, I would have great difficulty honoring or worshiping a wishy-washy deity who changes the rules on me and then expects me to figure out when and why. The Lord God that I revere is the same all the time and in every situation. He is always fair, right, good, reliable and consistent. I deeply respect the spotless character and unchanging personality of God.

I think that's why I'm amazed that God—perfect in every possible way and knowing all things at any given moment—is even interested in me. But He is. He is interested in you, too. In His loving sovereignty (seems like an oxymoron, doesn't it?), He designed an innovative (and frankly, miraculous) way for me to communicate and live peacefully with Him. And now, because I've accepted His gracious offer of new life, absolutely nothing stands between us, not my humanness, my imperfection, my limitations, or the sin that separated us in the first place. "For God made Christ, who never sinned, to be the offering for our sin, so that we could be made right with God through Christ" (2 Cor. 5:21, *NLT*).

God sent His flawless Son, Jesus, as His exact representative into my imperfect surroundings in order to reconnect me to

Himself, the omnipotent Creator and heavenly Father. Such a costly solution to the *gap* problem between God and me! God might have gotten very pushy about it, yet He treats you and me—His human creations—with such incredible respect that instead He allows us to decide whether we want to accept His reconciliation proposal. God shows such compassionate understanding of our bottom-line dilemma: *He is perfect and we are not.* He provides our solution, and yet our refusal to believe and trust His provision is our deepest and basic sin. We *need* Him—and the good news is that He *wants* us and created a way for us to connect. My friend Mary Pierce, author of *When Did I Stop Being Barbie and Become Mrs. Potato Head?*, describes the really good news of God's provision this way:

> The freeing truth is this: it was for my freedom that Christ died. He died so that I could be free of the burden of guilt, of sin. . . . Free of replaying sins in my head and punishing myself, over and over, for my mistakes. . . . Free of the rules, from having to perform to earn his love.[3]

The apostle John recorded Jesus as saying that the Holy Spirit will "show them that their refusal to believe in me is their basic sin" (John 16:9, *THE MESSAGE*). That's the key, you see. In order to connect with God, we simply stop refusing.

Here's the ultimate relief of imperfection: When you and I acknowledge our need and internally agree to partner with Him, the perfectionistic-shaped gap that kept us apart no longer exists. Yet inexplicably, we still often try to do it just right. Like Mary Alice Commeau, a real-estate asset manager, shares, we *can* acknowledge our need and *enjoy* the freedom and joy of knowing God personally:

"Mom, you've got to stop doing this. You're squeezing all the fun out of life. Give it up," begged my kids. "The house is clean already!"

Yet my life was out of control and I felt I *had* to control something. So I awoke at 4:00 A.M. each morning and worked continuously to perfect my surroundings, silently hoping it would quiet my inner chaos and help my marriage. The house did look nice, but I was a slave to it. I did not enjoy my life and certainly didn't feel free.

Then while trying to navigate through my divorce, a friend introduced me to Christ. Gradually I have learned to accept God's love and I *am* changing. I chuckle when I realize that my house is still clean, but I'm no longer a fanatic about it. It's an ongoing process and God is gently weaning me from my perfectionistic mindset. I know that God views me as "good" through Christ's work on my behalf—and that God doesn't expect me to appear perfect all the time.

Previously I couldn't even play a Dominos game without feeling I *must* win. Caring friends told me I was far too serious and showed me I could have and *be* fun even without winning. They were right. Imagine that!

I began to relax as I realized that I don't have to work so hard to do what is impossible to do anyway—chalk up increasing points with God. He doesn't expect me to be flawless. He loves me no matter what. Another revolutionary thought for me.

Although I've experienced numerous disappointments, it seems that with each one, a little piece of the old unrealistic me falls away and the real me emerges. Now I love to share this freeing reality with others— even though I know their experiences differ from mine.

I'm just grateful that I now have the energy and time I
formerly spent trying so hard to be perfect.

And No!

To be human is to be caught in ambiguity.
On the one hand, we were created to rule over the planet
in benevolent stewardship. On the other hand, we forfeited that right
when our forebears disobeyed God, and left us as a flawed, fallen race
which sees its potential but never quite reaches it.
RICHARD PEACE, *LEARNING TO LOVE OURSELVES* [4]

God doesn't expect you and me to be perfect, since He knows
our inherent limitations, neediness and faults. Psalm 103:14
says that God "knows how we are formed, he remembers that
we are dust." He accepts our humanness, even when we don't.

Although you and I might *long* to live beyond our limitations
of time, space, skin and finite reasoning, it isn't possible. We cannot completely halt the aging process. (Though I admit I do try
to hide its progress!) We cannot be two places at the same time.
(With six grandchildren under the age of seven, this would be
helpful!) We cannot live and thrive without sleep, rest, exercise
and human interaction. (Just think how much more I could accomplish if I didn't have to stop to sleep at night or answer the telephone!) We cannot read another's thoughts or change someone
else's beliefs or behavior. (But if I just knew what my husband
was thinking, I could spend less energy guessing!) We cannot fly
without an airplane. We cannot make a flower, cloud or mountain just by thinking about it. We cannot figure out all the answers
to life's messy predicaments. We cannot stop war, abuse or evil.
(Every rapid-fire newscast confirms this sobering truth.)

Our Creator knows all this, yet He has no unrealistic expectations for you and me. He just expects us to be the person He

designed us to be. This is not only feasible but reachable, because it is natural. He understands us and expects us only to trust Him and follow our unique God-given talents, gifts, values and desires. This down-to-earth process includes our calm, intentional pursuit of spiritual, intellectual, social and emotional growth. It fits you. It fits me. You and I don't have to be something or someone we're not. Which means I can release the tension in my shoulders just a little bit more!

What Does God Want?

Recently during my journaling time, I asked, "Lord, what do You want from me?" Startled by the immediate response I sensed within, I wrote:

> Joan, I want your heart. I want *you*. I know you're not perfect. You're not Super-Woman. I know you are human, limited and often needy. I know you sometimes doubt and have trouble trusting Me. I know you get confused, tired, feel inadequate, embarrassed and even ashamed sometimes. I know you're hurt when others can't or won't listen and then make assumptions about you. I know you try to understand others but get frustrated when you don't.
>
> I know you expect a lot. I know that you believe you *should* have more energy, better health and greater influence than you do. I know you can become self-preoccupied. And I know you want to make a significant difference in your world and that you're annoyed when you're limited by your need for sleep, rest, nourishment, exercise and social breaks. I know you want to be and do more.
>
> *Hmmm, Lord . . . You know all that?*

Yes, of course. I also know that your heart really loves Me and that you long to know and love Me more deeply. I know you want to grow, but sometimes you try too hard and that backfires on you.

Remember: I want your heart. I love *you*—not merely what you can do. You're My child. I'm your Father. I want you to grow. And since you want that, also, we're on the same page with this desire. I don't expect you to be, do or make it all *just right* all the time. That's My job.

In fact, let me assure you of this: When Jesus represented Me on Earth, He said, "Be perfect, therefore, as your heavenly Father is perfect" (Matt. 5:48). I realize those words may be a little confusing to you, so together let's investigate what they really mean.

I relished God's invitation to show me what Jesus meant by His "be perfect" talk during the Sermon on the Mount, and we got started immediately.

Although I can't read the original New Testament Scriptures (looks like Greek to me!), I talked with others who do know Greek and then studied from Greek-English dictionaries. I discovered that the word "perfect" means to be *complete, full-grown, developing*.

> And if you greet only your brothers, what are you doing more than others? Do not even pagans do that? Be perfect, therefore, as your heavenly Father is perfect (Matt. 5:47-48).

Re-reading this passage armed with my new vocabulary, it seems as though Jesus was and is urging you and me to grow past our stagnant religiosity and emotional status quo and be mature women. Advance past emotional and spiritual child-hood and adolescence. Live authentically and with integrity (the same on the inside as on the outside). Commit to growth and then practice following through, just as God consistently follows through with us. Be dedicated to completeness as God is complete.

Dr. Luke (author of the Gospel of Luke) wrote that Jesus also said, "Be merciful, just as your Father is merciful" (6:36). I think these verses in Luke and Matthew are related—scriptural kissing cousins, so to speak. Jesus seems to be urging us to listen and follow carefully—He's repeating and expanding on His directive. He's introducing a spiritual reality that the religious leaders of that time didn't usually practice. Most teachings emphasized loving your friends (those you agree with) and actively opposing and/or looking down on those who believe or behave differently than you.

> Love your enemies, do good to them, and lend to them without expecting to get anything back. Then your reward will be great, and you will be sons of the Most High, because he is kind to the ungrateful and wicked. Be merciful, just as your Father is merciful (Luke 6:35-36).

Jesus' revolutionary lectures on the mountainside challenged the current status quo. *Be unique, surprise your opponents,* He urged. *Respond to life and others with energy, concern and caring that is beyond you. Be merciful and complete, letting it flow from the presence of God, who resides within. It's an issue of the heart—not just how things look. It's not based on trying to do and look just right. Nor is it focused solely on appearing perfectly spiritual or religiously correct. It is a* heart *thing, and it comes from your close relationship with God.*

Sit with Your Desire

Delight yourself in the LORD
and he will give you the desires of your heart.
PSALM 37:4

Carol Travilla, my friend and co-author of *The Intentional Woman*, shared one of her trying-too-hard experiences with me. Several years ago while on a personal retreat, she met with a spiritual director to interact about her deep desire to experience God more intimately. "What does God want?" she asked her spiritual advisor. "Tell me what I'm doing right so that I can do more. And at the same time, show me what I might be doing wrong."

After listening intently, her spiritual companion replied, "Carol, I know you deeply desire to know God better. You're obviously passionate about being more intimate with Him. Just sit with that desire. Stay quiet. Listen, experience and enjoy being with God and your desire." I've never forgotten that relief-filled phrase: *Just sit with your desire.* It's an idea that was totally familiar to the composer of Psalm 42:1-2: "As the deer pants for streams of water, so my soul pants for you, O God. My soul thirsts for God, for the living God."

"Do you find yourself caught in a performance trap, where no matter what you do it doesn't seem to be enough? . . . Please listen carefully: That's not God's standard or expectation; it's someone else's. God doesn't enslave his sons and daughters; he frees them and enables them to serve. Don't keep trying to measure up to a standard that's not his. . . . Oh, what a relief it will be!"

Steve Brown, *Jumping Hurdles, Hitting Glitches, Overcoming Setbacks*[5]

God loves and partners with us in spite of our humanness, limitations, flaws, neediness, misconceptions and personality quirks. We need not be perfectly good, right or healthy in order to help, love, teach or serve. Kelli Gotthardt, an Intentional Woman presenter, a Christian yoga instructor, and a wife and mother, learned this difficult lesson through a long process of pain and shame. Here is her story:

> Over the years I've worked diligently to develop spiritual and emotional integrity. I admitted and worked through my eating disorder problems, people-pleasing philosophy and perfectionistic approach to life and ministry. But then a careless, inappropriate comment from a family member propelled me into deep darkness again. It dredged up old pain and exposed unhealthy patterns in my current life. I felt betrayed, cheapened and quite frustrated. *How dare he do that? It just isn't right!*
>
> I committed to more internal work, which cost time, energy and money. It was worth it—I found fresh insights, new ways of relating to people and a more intimate, authentic relationship with God. However, I felt unable to forgive the one who had ignited this painful process and uncomfortable with the previously hidden anger it exposed.
>
> So I prayed, "Lord, I know You've sent this trial to make me a more perfect reflection of You in the ministry You've given me. I know I must get over this unforgiveness and anger before You can use me again. Please help me."
>
> But my anger seemed to increase in direct relation to my heightened cries for God to fix me. I did everything I knew how to do (counseling, difficult conversations, Scripture, prayer, spiritual direction) and I could not achieve the perfection I desired. I wanted to face an

audience and share my victory over unforgiveness—to announce with conviction that with God's power, we can fix anything and everything. "After all, that's the allure of Christianity," I reasoned.

Yet I got more and more tired trying to make it all right—my emotions, my soul, my head, my relationships, my family, my ministry. It was like trying to hold back the dam. I couldn't keep up anymore. But when I released control, something surprising happened.

One day at dawn I awoke crying because I was invited to pray with our state's governor and I didn't feel my life was *together* enough. That same night, I fell asleep crying for joy, because I felt overwhelmed at God's love and willingness to use my imperfection.

Now I feel released to do whatever God leads me to do without having to be perfect first. This is new thinking for me—freeing *and* uncomfortable. I don't really know how this will affect the people I minister to, but I do know it has profoundly changed how I interact with God. It's another huge step in my process of ceasing to *earn* His favor. And the less I try to earn it, the more I'm free to just love Him. How liberating!

Kelli shared with me her journal entry from that transformational day in her life. Perhaps you can identify with her truth-filled yet freeing insights. She wrote:

Lord, I have so much shame about not being perfect. I don't want to be in need of forgiveness. Seems some of my anger directly connects to my constant frustration with not being able to obtain perfection. I've tried and tried and I can't get it all together. Here I am, imperfect, desperately dependent, humbly insufficient. Although I strive to be all fixed, I'm not. I feel broken and very tired.

Yet I don't want to live in constant fear of making a mistake. So I'm going to stop beating myself up for being human and just acknowledge my dependence on You. I bring my driven-to-perfection-ness and drop it at Your feet. It's too heavy for me. I feel myself breathing easier now.

Yes to an Imperfect Partnership

Even if you live a long time, don't take a single day for granted.
Take delight in each light-filled hour . . . Honor and enjoy your Creator.
ECCLESIASTES 11:7-8; 12:1, *THE MESSAGE*

It is God's plan to partner with sinful, flawed, limited human beings who choose to follow His Son, Jesus Christ. During His 33 years on Earth, Jesus surrounded Himself with perfectly imperfect people who decided to admit their needs, take risks, make mistakes and grow. These are the kind of people who formed His ministry team. Actually, He didn't spend much time with those who feigned perfection, appeared on top of it all, made unreasonable religious rules, blamed others for their dilemmas and remained preoccupied with appearances. Instead He preferred working, playing and living with people just like you and me. He enjoyed imperfect partnerships back then, just as He does today. What a relief!

You amaze me, Lord.
In love and grace You created me and bridged
the perfectionistic-shaped gap between us.
I know You never forget who I am and where I came from.
Thank You for affirming my heart's desire to partner with You
and for inviting me to sit and enjoy Your company.
As I linger here with You, my persistently nagging shame fades.
I can't stop smiling.

CHAPTER 3

When Playing God Is No Longer My Best Role

The problem . . . is not that we cannot do it all,
but that we want to do it all.
I am increasingly convinced that many
of our guilt feelings
are based on our Messianic aspirations,
our desire to be God and take over his work.
Henri Nouwen[1]

While taking an afternoon walk, I noticed several white bell-shaped flowers clinging to the straggly weeds along a hidden trail. "What a shame the beauty and fragrance of these flowers is wasted on this secluded spot," I thought. "They'd show better in my yard with the geraniums, marigolds, petunias and ferns. I wonder if anyone else has noticed them here."

"God has," said a small voice inside my mind. I smiled sheepishly. There I go again. Trying to maneuver even nature to be better and more effective.

Months later during another walk, I once again tried to unravel my world's knotty problems. I sorted through the various schemes in my head and felt my neck tighten with each just-try-harder plan I devised. Then a thought jolted me to a swift stop. *Joan, you think you know what's best for your family, husband, children, colleagues and friends. But here's a newsflash for you:*

You don't! When you try to figure out others' motives, thoughts and solutions, you're dangerously close to playing God. Give yourself a break. It's not your job.

Longing to Help

You don't really need to be God. That job is already filled.
ENID HOWARTH AND JAN TRAS, THE JOY OF IMPERFECTION[2]

As caring and discerning women, we may have useful suggestions for other people and their sticky situations. We're privileged to share these ideas with them at appropriate times. Yet sometimes we slide over the line and operate out of a distorted sense of responsibility. We may mistakenly believe it is our duty to see into another person's mind and heart—because we think we know others' needs or feelings, we assume we can handle their dilemmas. "You should take this job" or "You'll be sorry if you marry this guy" or "Don't attend that secular university" or "You'd better see a doctor; I'll make the appointment" are examples of our I-know-a-better-way thinking.

Nancy Kennedy, author of *When Perfect Isn't Enough*, is all too familiar with the temptation. She writes, "In my home, I have labored in vain whenever I've tried to do God's job: convicting of sin, changing hearts. I also labor in vain when I lie awake worrying about things I cannot control."[3]

We really do long to help, yet sometimes our helping crosses the boundary into God's territory. We may honestly believe we know what medicine Tom should take, what Bible study our neighbor must try, and how Sue and Jim should solve their marriage problems. Some of us verbalize our solutions, while others of us hold our perceptive thoughts close to our hearts and get edgy when the other person doesn't figure it out. It's time to write ourselves a little reminder note: *You are not in charge of the universe; you are in charge of yourself.*[4]

Gasping for Air!

Trust GOD from the bottom of your heart;
don't try to figure out everything on your own . . .
Don't assume that you know it all. Run to GOD! . . .
Your body will glow with health, your very bones will vibrate with life!
PROVERBS 3:5-8, *THE MESSAGE*

When in this over-responsibility mode, we sometimes forget to breathe. (*Yikes!* Not good!) It's hard to relax when our personal satisfaction hinges on a loved one's attitudes or actions. *Doesn't she know it could work better if she just had a different attitude or plan? Doesn't he get it?* Or perhaps someone we barely know—a clerk, a fellow church member, a doctor's assistant—neglects to return our call or give us the info we need. *It's not that difficult. How could she do that? Doesn't he know I've got a deadline?*

If you're a little muddled about how trying too hard, perfectionism and playing God are linked, you're not alone. I'm often puzzled, too. Even experts get confused trying to sort all this out.[5] On occasion, God splashes light into my fogginess through humorous life predicaments. Because all the universe is under God's domain, I've discovered He can use anything to teach, nurture and grow me. (I love how He does that!) Sometimes new insight comes from surprising venues.

Like that *aha!* moment I had while watching the movie *Driving Miss Daisy* a few years ago. The wealthy Miss Daisy and her longtime chauffeur have both aged considerably. As they discuss their situations, Miss Daisy accuses the chauffeur of continuing to drive even though his eyesight is failing. "How do you know how I can see, 'lessen you look out my eyes?" is his response.[6]

My internal reaction: *Whoa! Lord, forgive me for thinking I'm powerful enough to know another's needs. I realize I will never see their life from their view. I want to learn to treat others with respect. Please help me.*

The apostle Paul, in his first letter to the Corinthians, cautions us about assuming we know another's thoughts and feelings: "No one can really know what anyone else is thinking, or what he is really like, except that person himself" (1 Cor. 2:11, *TLB*).

Recently I read some material by Dr. Monica Ramirez Basco that helped me wrap some words around this perfectionistic mindset. Although this trying-too-hard-to-make-it-just-right approach has many faces, it seems to fall into two basic categories of perfectionism: *internally* directed and *externally* directed. Basco, author of *Never Good Enough*, writes, "Inwardly focused perfectionists hide what they believe are their incompetencies by working very hard, but still fear that at some point, someone will figure out that they are not what they seem to be. Outwardly focused perfectionists . . . are frustrated with the people in their world, feel a loss of control over their lives or their family, or feel angry that things in their lives are not turning out the right way."[7]

Internally directed perfectionists fear they might do it wrong, causing others and God to disapprove. The *it* that they might do incorrectly may include relationships, jobs, projects, parenting, prayer, Bible Study, love, church or marriage. Externally directed perfectionists, on the other hand, might admit that another person, group, church or organization is not perfect, yet they tenaciously (and sometimes unknowingly) adhere to the belief that they *should* be. *If others would just do what I want—when I want and in the way I prefer—then everything would work out fine and I'd be more peaceful.*

"The secret of my success is that at an early age I discovered I was not God."

Supreme Court Justice Oliver Wendell Holmes, Jr.

Both internally and externally directed perfectionists espouse anxiety-producing misbeliefs that rob them of the joy and intimacy they crave. Basco continues, "Many people have characteristics of both types depending on the situation."[8] The relief-filled truth is: We can progressively release our need to do it just right by taking intentional steps to trust God for what is not ours to control or direct. Then we can enjoy living in the freedom and grace He patiently waits to give us.

A Disturbing Dilemma

A relaxed attitude lengthens life.
PROVERB 14:30, *NLT*

Not all of us are perfectionists in every area of our lives, but research indicates that most of us either exhibit occasional perfectionist tendencies or live with someone who does. Bestselling author Dr. David Seamands maintains that "perfectionism is the most disturbing emotional problem among evangelical Christians."[9] Throughout this book, you'll learn more about the various versions of perfectionism with its subtle symptoms, characteristics and misbeliefs. You'll also gain relief-producing insights into how to let God be God in your daily endeavors and opportunities. You'll read stories like this one from my talented and humorous sister, Patty Brock (a wife, mother and business owner), as well as from other women—including me—who realize that *playing God* is no longer our best role:

> Apparently someone (no names!) thought a story from me might be appropriate for this playing-God chapter of her book. And why not? For years she's watched me attempt to have all the answers for everyone who needed

a solution (or not). I wanted to make everything right and good—and help everyone *be* better.

What's wrong with that? I felt it was the loving, giving, Christian thing to do. And lest I sound facetious, I assure you my conscious motive was to be the best Christian I could by recognizing how my ideas and actions influenced and directed others. As early as I can remember, I desired to help the weak and hurting, fix the broken and right any wrong (as God and I viewed it). This seemed to work well—it suited my outgoing, persuasive personality and my gifts of leadership and administration. *Hey, is it okay to write this for all to see?*

Through the years I'm sure some people merely tolerated my verbal wisdom (mixed with a little advice and personal opinion!). Yet most seemed to *seek* my advice, especially during my 10 single years. This reinforced the notion that everyone needed me, or at least a part of me. I experienced an adrenaline rush when I helped someone, yet at the same time felt the burden of responsibility and it weighed heavy.

Then came marriage! *Wow!* I didn't know what overload really felt like until I married my husband and focused on making him and us just right. I felt responsible for assuring his happiness, choices, growth and success. Why did I ever think I could pull that off? I guess down deep I knew I couldn't, but I still tried. The repeated result included frustration and disappointment, even though I felt I was doing what God wanted me to do.

Then came children—two boys and two girls! I dedicated myself to cheerfully meeting all their needs. Consumed with making each child happy every minute, my brain often felt like it would explode. As the kids grew older, I continued to believe I was supposed to fix every situation that was less than perfect—their choices, relationships and daily activities. *Certainly God would help me do just that!* Yet as the children started graduating and heading to college, God gradually began to show me where my responsibility ended and His began.

After some painful events that resulted in new insight, I recently read *Boundaries* by Dr. Henry Cloud and Dr. John Townsend. In this book, they write, "Just as homeowners set physical property lines around their land, we need to set mental, physical, emotional, and spiritual boundaries for our lives to help us distinguish what is our responsibility and what isn't."[10] I now recognize that I do *not* have to bear the responsibility for anyone other than myself. Everything does *not* hinge on what I do or don't do. I am *not* responsible for anyone's decisions, nor is it my job to fix them or the situations they encounter as a result of their choices. *What a novel idea!*

The cool part is: I don't even *want* to do that anymore. I know I can't. Life is way too big for me or my capabilities, yet nothing is too big for God. I don't have to struggle to make things work just right for everyone. I'm finding new freedom and I'm grateful!

When Nice Becomes Control

Carmen Renee Berry, author of *When Helping You Is Hurting Me,* writes, "It's easy to get confused by the Messiah Trap, a two-sided lie that, on the surface, appears to be noble, godly, and gracious. After all, being a caring and helpful person is something we value."[11] Berry suggests that we believe one of two lies when we get caught in this trap.

Messiah Trap Lie Number One: *If I don't do it, it won't get done.* Messiah Trap people are doers, helpers and genuinely nice people. We keep homes and offices running smoothly. But we can become weary and overwhelmed when we believe another person's happiness, spirituality, health and/or success is our God-given task. Berry says, "The Messiah Trap is an odd combination of feeling grandiose yet worthless, of being needed and yet abandoned, of playing God while groveling."[12]

"I believe the fantasy of unlimited human power to control is the most primitive and intensely cherished illusion of all people, children or adults. This belief convinces people that they have the power to cause events and control people."

Sandra D. Wilson, *The World According to Me*[13]

Maybe this applies to you. Maybe it doesn't. But before you write it off, consider this: What if a friend, colleague, spouse or child fails to live up to your idea, dream or suggestion for him? If your plan doesn't pan out, do you feel like a failure? Make excuses for the other person? Sometimes when caught in the Messiah Trap, we feel embarrassed and believe another's poor choices reflect negatively on our own level of success, growth or spirituality.

Messiah Trap Lie Number Two: *Everyone else's needs should take priority over mine*. Because we don't want to be or appear selfish, we often neglect our own spiritual, emotional, medical or social needs. People depend on us for answers and unending support, which makes us feel important and worthwhile. However, when inevitable humanness breaks through our facade, we may find no one to help us. We can then feel isolated, lonely or disillusioned.

It's a catch-22, because we dislike the imperfect sensation associated with insignificance or disappointment almost as much as we dislike losing control and not making everything just right. These less-than-perfect emotions and experiences feel so miserable that we deduce we must try harder to avoid feeling this way. Or we withdraw, pretending we never experienced the uncomfortable feelings in the first place. Either way, it is a genuine relief once we realize that God doesn't expect us to have all the answers in order to be a valuable and compassionate friend, wife, mother, colleague or Christian. "Relax, everything's going to be all right; rest, everything's coming together; open your hearts, love is on the way!" (Jude 2, *THE MESSAGE*).

No Omnipotent Human Beings

Recently I asked several writer friends how they define the phrase "playing God." Mary Pierce, author of *When Did My Life Become a Game of Twister?* said, "Playing God is trying to manipulate events or people to make certain that things come out right—or the way I want them to. We play God when we adhere to the my-way-or-the-highway philosophy. For example: helicopter parents who hover over their children and all their activities and relationships. It's trying to be all things to all people. Omniscient! Omnipresent! Omnipotent! Hey, now *that's* playing God."

In Mary's book, *Confessions of a Prayer Wimp*, she has a chapter titled "Hand Over the Metal Bra and Nobody Gets Hurt." She describes how she wanted to say yes when offered a well-paying speaking engagement, but because of writing deadlines, an ill family member and other circumstances, she knew she must say no. She didn't want to disappoint anyone, so she agonized for days because she couldn't be all those places at once. Mary admits she wants to be "Wonder Woman. But maybe without the metal bra."[14] She goes on to say, "Just because people request our time and energy doesn't mean we have to say yes. We can follow Jesus' example and decline the invitation.

Does this mean we turn into self-absorbed, self-centered jerks? Did Jesus? I think not!"[15]

"What does playing God mean to you?" I asked while dining with my friend Marsha Crockett, author of *Break Through: Unearthing God's Image to Find the Real You.*

"Playing God happens when I sense that someone I care about is unhappy and I automatically deduce I must have done something wrong. Like I have that much power! It can also happen when we transfer our own (often unrealistic) expectations onto others—expectations for their behavior and attitudes. We feel embarrassed by their actions because we believe what they do makes us look bad. It's quite uncomfortable for us, so we remain strongly convinced we *must* save them from further mistakes."

Marsha and I agreed that a truly loving (yet admittedly difficult) action would be to step back and let those we care about experience the consequences of their own decisions. Then God can step in at the point of their felt need. Marsha reflects on the difficulty of choosing between control and letting go in her book *Dancing in the Desert*:

> "Failure is not an option." This phrase, made popular by the heroic mission of Apollo 13, reminds us that we can accomplish anything we set our minds to—even reach the moon. Our ingenuity enables us to conquer all obstacles at any expense. . . . [But] if "failure is not an option," then what are we to do with the reality of our mistakes and fallen expectations?[16]

Leaving Control Freakdom

Debbie Gilster, a business owner, wife, mother and ministry volunteer, admits her propensity to be a control freak. "But I want to stop trying to do it all and be it all," she shared recently as we discussed her story:

> As a child, I learned not to trust other people. Why bother? Based on experience, I knew they wouldn't stick around. By the time I was in my early 20s, Mother was in her fourth marriage and Dad in his third.
>
> "If I'm extra good, perhaps they won't leave me," I reasoned. So I tried to do everything *best*. I got exceptional grades, helped Mom around the house, babysat my younger brother and sister, and excelled in many school activities. I became a Girl Scout, class officer, cheerleader and member of the tennis team. I even lost a lot of weight. I did all this in a determined effort to control the outcome I wanted: *Now they won't leave me.*
>
> I didn't know it until recently, but to compensate for my lack of trust, I became a control freak. I figure that if I control the situation, I'll also control the outcome. I create environments and systems where everything is perfect. Surely people (including God) will be *so* happy and impressed with my accomplishments that they'll say, "Wow! Debbie is great. We need her. She is indispensable."
>
> I viewed failing as a sign of weakness. Who wants to be around a failure? Out of fear that everyone would walk away and I'd be alone again (couldn't let that happen!), I planned and re-planned my life and everyone else's. (Or at least I'd show them how by solving, helping, controlling, fixing problems.) I even became a professional organizer!
>
> Although I felt abandoned during my not-so-positive life experiences (unstable parental systems, abusive alcoholic stepfather, hearing loss, missing front tooth dur-

ing grade school, date rape and, recently, the loss of a prestigious position), I now know God was here all along and waiting for me to partner with Him. Not as an afterthought, but all the time. I used to plan first and then pray for approval. After working through the Intentional Woman five-step process, I began to change the way I think and strategize.[17] Now I pray for guidance first, believing that God has a good plan and that He'll share it with me. I want to release my need to control it all (made me too tired, anyway).

God grants me peace when I turn from trying to do it just right all alone and release my next steps to Him. I'm discovering that when I lower the intensity on my control-the-future dial, I am happier, more relaxed and even more organized. As a recovering control freak, it is not always easy. This is new territory for me. So I'm learning to take it one step at a time.

Releasing God's Role

Perhaps you picture "playing God" as a role performed by doctors, scientists, governments and insurance companies when they make life-altering decisions or laws concerning medical treatment, abortion, cloning, and death and dying issues. These may be not-so-subtle ways that humans attempt to usurp their Creator's wise authority, yet many of us play God in subtler ways. We have an idea and it just *must* be executed—for the good of others, our sense of serenity and God's honor. We may have trouble conceiving that there is another option or goal than ours, or that God is at work in the painful circumstances we're determined to avoid.

Recently I pressed hard to figure out what went haywire between a friend and me. I walked the streets of my neighborhood begging God to show me. *Please help, Lord. Take away this tension and ache.* As I increased my silent prayer intensity, I walked faster and faster. Then God seemed to whisper, although not audibly, "Joan, it's okay. Don't fight this. I'm doing something here. Trust Me." While still sad and hurt, it was what I needed to stop my internal thrashing and release the tension-filled situation to Him. Relief! I didn't have to figure it out or fix it.

This reminds me of an interaction between Peter and Jesus (see Matt. 16:21-23). "I want you to know that in a few days I'm going to be killed," said Jesus.

Upon hearing these words, Peter decided he'd better have a talk with Jesus. "There's no way we can let this happen to you," he said.

Jesus immediately responded, "Peter, you think you're helping, but you're actually hindering Me. My Father is doing something here. Stop trying to be bigger than God."

"We need control in our lives. The problem is when the good qualities start to bleed into areas where we have no right to control and we start to control other peoples' lives or try to control circumstances that are beyond our control. One of my tenets is everybody is somebody's control freak some of the time."

Les Parrot, PhD, in "The Anatomy of Control," an interview by Joseph R. Dunn, PhD[18]

Like Peter, we choose to follow Jesus and want God's purposes fulfilled on Earth. As Peter did, we may attempt to step in and figure out a perfect solution, protecting another from pending hurt or preventing a shaky situation from becoming disastrous (in our opinion). In doing so, we might hinder God's strategy for insight and growth in another's life, or in our church or organization. We cannot always know God's agenda for another's spiritual maturity or how God purposes to show His power. Peter's interference could have blocked the fulfillment of God's mission for Jesus—and our salvation.

For many years in my marriage, I felt restricted. To me it seemed that my husband, Richard, attempted to control what I wore and how I looked, what I did and what I believed, what we purchased, where we went and who we went with. Appearing like the perfect couple and family seemed to be more important than individual growth or contentment. I did everything I could to make him happy. But I burned out and decided I didn't want to live this way anymore.

I began to change the way I interacted with Richard, although it was extremely difficult for me. Gathering miniscule bits of courage, I shared my hurts, needs and desires. At first he was flabbergasted because he didn't know I felt "squashed." It would have been more comfortable and certainly a lot less frightening for me to just give up and return to our old system of relating. But I had come far enough to taste inner freedom and I couldn't retreat to the internal prison I allowed.

What I learned shocked me. I, the controlled, was also a controller. I tried to manage (a nice word for control) his reactions or moods by making our life work just right and appear just *so*. In order to win his approval, I hid what I really thought and what I honestly needed. I wanted to keep him upbeat, happy and satisfied with life, so I did everything and anything I could do to avoid his displeasure, disappointment or discontent. If the mail brought unpleasant news or an unwanted bill, I hid it with the intention of taking care of it myself so that he wouldn't have to deal with it. If the kids misbehaved, I tried to smooth it over so that he wouldn't be disappointed in them or me. I overworked and stayed up late to get the household duties, correspondence and finances figured out so that I wouldn't have to deal with these things on his time off.

When it dawned on me that I had tried to control Richard and his reactions, I wept. I had engaged in a form of lying by *not* telling him my genuine desires, needs, goals and God-given calling, and it was a bitter discovery. (Even now it stings to admit it.) I wasn't honoring God's wise directives to "speak the truth in love" (see Eph. 4:15). I avoided admitting and sharing the truth (even to myself) if it appeared hurtful, negative or unpleasant. This was not what God wanted for me, who He designed me to be or what He created me to do. I truly wanted to change—and I did.

And I deeply respect Richard for staying and changing with me. Though it was extremely uncomfortable at first, Richard heard my feeble attempts to share my hurts with him. He listened, apologized and worked with me to adjust the faulty system that valued perfect appearances over authentic love. Although we never stopped loving one another, I was angry at the injustice I felt. We didn't always know how to verbalize our thoughts or emotions—and still don't. We're imperfect people in an imperfect world, on an ongoing journey of growth, partnership and love. He is my number one supporter and a consistent help with the nitty-gritty stuff of life, such as grocery shopping, running errands, laundry and paying the bills. He applauds my victories and I rejoice in his. I cherish him even more than I did that New Year's Eve many years ago when we both said "I do."

I admit I'm still sometimes confused and uncertain about what is right, wrong or in-between. Yet with each new God-inspired insight, I gain understanding and courage to move away from my restrictive black-or-white thinking—my attempts to play God—and into the colorful and spacious arena of options, renegotiation and release.

Relaxing with God's Role

He brought me out into a spacious place;
he rescued me because he delighted in me.
PSALM 18:19

God has supreme power, authority and creativity. Out of His vast resources, God lovingly gives us the ability to reason, choose, plan and implement those plans. In this reality we can relax, trusting Him to help us make wise decisions and live reasonable, loving and peaceful lives. He invites us to join Him in this theater of life. What a relief-filled privilege it is to do life with God in the leading role!

> If God gives such attention to the appearance of wildflowers—most of which are never even seen—don't you think he'll attend to you, take pride in you, do his best for you? What I'm trying to do here is to get you to relax . . . Steep your life in God-reality, God-initiative, God-provisions (Matt. 6:30-33, *THE MESSAGE*).

Lord,
You created me; I did not create You.
You sustain me; I do not sustain my world.
I release my lofty attempts to play Your role.
I'll never do this perfectly,
so please nudge me when I start to upstage You.
I don't want to do that anymore.
You lovingly care for each wildflower and
I believe You'll take care of me, too.
How grateful I am to be sharing life with You,
now and forever.

Relief Reminder

Before reading the next section, "The Relief of Imperfect Relationships and Families," take a break and play (not *work*!) through the Relief Guide for "What's Wrong with Perfection?" You may do it alone or invite someone to join you.

What's Wrong with Perfection?

God will take care of your tomorrow, too.
Live one day at a time.
Matthew 6:34, *TLB*

Now that you've finished reading chapters 1 through 3 of *The Relief of Imperfection*, I invite you to answer the questions and complete the exercises below in your Relief Journal. Remember that you always have the option to respond *Yes*, *No*, *Renegotiate* or *Later*. (See "Read This First!" for more explanation about these options.)

1. What caused you to pick up and start reading *The Relief of Imperfection*?

2. With which story, anecdote or illustration in chapters 1, 2 and 3 do you most identify? In what way?

3. Read the following quote. What's your spontaneous reaction?

   Perfectionism is everyone's issue. We inhale it with the air pollution. We swim in it. Perfectionism grabs us whenever we curse ourselves for being wrong, being late, being dumb. It haunts us when we know we could and should have done better, understood everything, and predicted all the consequences.[1]

4. To help you assess your expectations and level of perfectionistic tendency in specific areas of your life right now, complete the following *Relief of Imperfection* Awareness Wheel. The six life areas you're measuring compare to the six "reliefs" in this book. They include:

- *Relationships and families:* friends, children, in-laws, grandchildren, extended family, spouse, dating

- *Emotions, minds and bodies:* physical, emotional and mental well-being, health and body image issues, exercise, soul-care, journaling, education

- *Life-work and service:* employment, career including full-time mother or homemaker, home-schooling, avocation/volunteer work

- *Churches and culture:* church work, worship time, ministry, church leaders, missionary and charity affiliations, media, societal pressures, community/neighborhood

- *Dreams, plans and decisions:* current, future and former plans, choices, vision, purposes, opportunities

- *Faith, prayer and spirituality:* quiet times, prayer life, Bible study, relationship with God, spiritual formation

Relief of Imperfection Awareness Wheel
Figure 1—Example

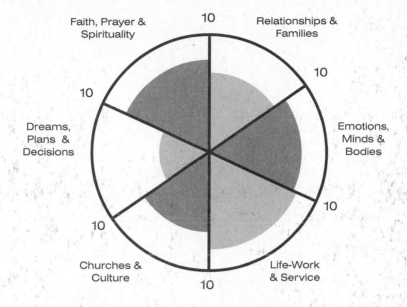

There's no perfect way to do your Wheel. It's for your awareness. Take a breath, have fun and share your discoveries!

A. In or near each wedge of the wheel on Figure 2, write one to three expectations you have for that area of your life. For example, "I should have a 45 minute Quiet Time each day" or "My child will make the honor roll" or "I'll always meet a deadline" or "Parents must always agree."

B. With the center of the wheel as 0 and the outer edge as 10, rank your current sense of pressure or overwhelm in that area by drawing a curved line from one side of the wedge to the other. Ask, *What is my current sense of perfectionistic overwhelm in this area?*

Relief of Imperfection Awareness Wheel
Figure 2—Your Turn

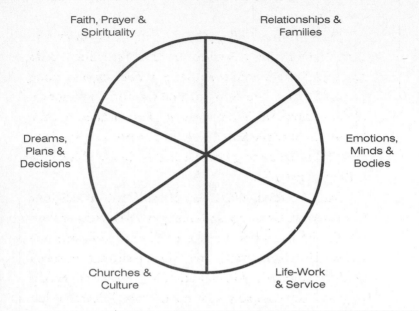

Faith, Prayer & Spirituality

Relationships & Families

Dreams, Plans & Decisions

Emotions, Minds & Bodies

Churches & Culture

Life-Work & Service

C. Shade the area from the center to your curved line to help you visualize your current "relief of imperfection" level (see example in Figure 1). Where are you already giving yourself relief-filled grace and space? In what areas are you sensing the pressure today?

D. What jumps out at you about your *Relief of Imperfection* Awareness Wheel? Jot down your discoveries in your Relief Journal. At the end of the book, you'll have the opportunity to re-do and follow-up on this Awareness Wheel. For now, it's "good enough." ☺

5. Read the following passage from Matthew 11:25-30:

Abruptly Jesus broke into prayer: "Thank you, Father, Lord of heaven and earth. You've concealed your ways from sophisticates and know-it-alls, but spelled them out clearly to ordinary people. Yes, Father, that's the way you like to work."

Jesus resumed talking to the people, but now tenderly. "The Father has given me all these things to do and say. This is a unique Father-Son operation, coming out of Father and Son intimacies and knowledge. No one knows the Son the way the Father does, nor the Father the way the Son does. But I'm not keeping it to myself; I'm ready to go over it line by line with anyone willing to listen.

"Are you tired? Worn out? Burned out on religion? Come to me. Get away with me and you'll recover your life. I'll show you how to take a real rest. Walk with me and work with me—watch how I do it. Learn the unforced rhythms of grace. I won't lay anything heavy or ill-fitting on you. Keep company with me and you'll learn to live freely and lightly" (*THE MESSAGE*).

Take a few moments to reflect on Jesus' words and to talk with God about what you're learning, sensing and/or feeling at the moment. To help you remember, I suggest you write your prayer in your journal and date it.

> *Lord, I've decided to partner with You one step at a time.*
> *Thank You for taking care of my concerns about tomorrow.*
> *When I start to worry and fear—and because I'm human, I will—*
> *please remind me that You're there.*
> *Trusting You is such a relief.*

That's it! Congratulations. You finished your first Relief Guide. During this week, share your discoveries with a friend, or turn to your group partner and tell her, "Way to go!"

The Relief of
Imperfect Relationships
and Families

CHAPTER 4

Joy! I Don't Have to Fix It All—Including You!

*Forget perfect. Establish and cherish
the good-enough relationship
by being a good-enough partner. Talk. Listen.
Laugh. . . . Avoid being disrespectful. . . .
Stay clear about what you like, what you want,
where you set your limits.
Be flexible. Adapt.*

Enid Howarth and Jan Tras, *The Joy of Imperfection*[1]

After concluding my presentation and dismissing the audience, several people walked toward me as I stood at the front of the room. One determined young woman reached me first. She said (loudly), "You're not going to like this, but . . ." Then she detailed the reasons she did not appreciate or agree with my talk.

My immediate response was, "Yes, but didn't you hear me mention . . . ?" I began to recount the points of my workshop. After all, I thought I had covered each of her verbal complaints. I felt we were on the same page, so I wanted to help her see that, too.

Then I noticed that instead of helping her understand, I compounded her agitation. Stopping mid-sentence, I said, "Basically, you didn't agree with anything I said, did you?"

Her face relaxed as she broke into a huge smile. "No, sorry. I didn't," she admitted and walked on.

One of the freedom-producing truths I am learning is that I am not responsible for another's reactions, whether that person is a close family member, friend, co-worker, fellow church member or someone I've never met before. I can express my thoughts and beliefs, but if someone else does not concur, I need not try to change her mind, manipulate her to agree . . . or silently judge her.

In my growing-up years, I developed (and carried into adulthood) the misbelief that I needed to have a solution to every (well, almost!) crisis, a reason for all behavior, the rationale for every emotion and the answer to every spiritual inquiry. Or at least try to. I felt I owed it to God and His reputation. With so much tragedy and pain in the world, I longed to be a part of the solution. (Still do.) Yet the strain of trying to always be strong and have the right answers all the time wore me out.

Released from Telling It All and Fixing It All

Always be prepared to give an answer to everyone who asks you
to give the reason for the hope that you have.
But do this with gentleness and respect.
1 PETER 3:15

I searched God's Word, looking for the promise of relief and found it in a surprising place: 1 Peter 3:15. I learned this verse in the *King James Version* and that's what kept running through my mind: "Be ready always to give an answer to every man that asketh you a reason of the hope that is in you." *Lord, if I must always be vigilant to have the solutions to everyone's questions, how can this bring me relief? After all, I think this verse is one of the reasons I'm in this predicament.*

Then I saw it! The phrases "*asketh* you" and "hope that is in *you*" jumped off the pages at me. They traveled from my head (where a lot of new information gets stuck!) down into my heart (where God's refreshing transformation starts). I found the relief I desired! (1) I don't have to provide answers or insights to those who don't ask or sense their need. (2) I don't need to give reasons for the *hope* (or spiritual experiences) of anyone else—my pastor, parents, Bible Study teacher or spouse—*only my own*. (3) I *do* have the privilege of sharing my own hope to those who are hungry and asking for input.

"To make relationships work, we need courage more than repair and love more than insight."

Dr. Larry Crabb, *Understanding Who You Are*[2]

Peter's words (which previously supported my be-on-constant-alert-with-all-the-right-answers-for-every-situation mode) now actually released me to relax, interact truthfully and trust God for the outcome. As I basked in my newfound insight, I read Peter's next phrase: "But do this with gentleness and respect." *Oh, I get it, Lord. The young woman who disagreed with my presentation walked away with a smile on her face and a bounce in her step because she felt heard and respected for her own thoughts, feelings and perceptions.*

Dr. Henry Cloud and Dr. John Townsend, in their book *Boundaries*, write, "We are not . . . responsible for other people. Nowhere are we commanded to have 'other-control,' although we spend a lot of time and energy trying to get it!"[3] I am responsible for myself, for what I choose to believe—not others' beliefs. I can share my experiences and the good news about who God is and how He rescues me. But I don't have to know it all, give it all, tell it all, teach it all or fix it all. (Oh, joy!)

Believing this can renew our lost energy, help restore our hurting relationships and reduce our opinionated approach to living the Christian life. Eventually (it's a process!) we'll be breathing easier, as Heather Washburn, a home-schooler and Bible teacher, confirms in her story:

I am a relational perfectionist. Over the years I worked diligently to make my husband happy and our marriage strong. Then my husband's discharge from 12 years of active military duty ushered him into an identity crisis, and no matter what I said or did, I couldn't convince him that he was still the wonderful man I married. I tried to. I directed every thought, action and effort to fix my husband and make him content. It didn't work. Distance grew between us.

At a desperately dark time when both my husband and I were tempted to have affairs, our marriage seemed over. I felt sick, hurt and rejected, just like I did when my father left my mom years ago. "Why, God?" I sobbed. "I've been trying to build this marriage for years. Why are you ripping it away?"

While I was curled up in the fetal position on the floor, God whispered to my heart, "Heather, I will never reject you."

That's when I realized: *Having a secure marriage was the focus of my life. My husband had the place of Christ in my affection.* That day, I surrendered my marriage to God, removed my husband as my idol and took Christ as my spiritual husband. After 13 years of trying, I finally knew I could never be enough to make our life perfect. I couldn't fix my husband or make him happy. I would no longer try to morph into what I thought he needed. He alone could make the choice to be happy.

Although not immediately released from the bondage I had known for years, surrendering began my imperfect journey to relationship freedom. As I realized I could never meet my husband's every need, I admitted he couldn't fulfill mine either. All my efforts never produced what I wanted anyway, so I stopped trying so hard to create the perfect marriage. I learned that no human being, regardless of how loving or committed (my husband is both), will ever provide the security I crave. Only Christ can.

After liberating my husband from meeting all my relational needs, God brought two amazing women into my life, filling a need for female companionship I never knew I had. Soon I detected old relational patterns sprouting up in these friendships. When I sensed distance or agitation between us, I tried too hard to fix it. I called often to make certain I hadn't offended them. This behavior didn't enhance either relationship. At least I caught it sooner this time. Now I know what to watch for. When I try to fix a relationship, person or experience and make everything perfect, I know I have a choice: I can keep squeezing or release. I choose the relief of release.

Did Jesus Fix It All?

Figure out what's broken and fix it. That's the way we naturally think. But that attitude reduces us to things like faucets that sometimes break and fail to function properly. . . . We are relational, not mechanical.

DR. LARRY CRABB, *WHO YOU ARE: WHAT YOUR RELATIONSHIPS TELL YOU ABOUT YOURSELF*[4]

"Excuse me, Sir. I've been watching you and I know you're a good teacher. So I have a question for you," said a successful young man (see Matt. 19:16-22). "I've been thinking and I'd really like to know what good, generous thing I can do to ensure I'll live forever."

"What causes you to ask this question?" responded Jesus. "There's only one who is inherently good and that is God Himself. Obey all His directives and you'll be guaranteed eternal life."

"Which ones do you mean?" asked the man. Jesus listed several commandments including the one to love others as he loved himself.

"I've got all that covered," said the affluent young man. "What else should I do?"

Jesus, knowing how to reach this man's bottom-line need, said, "Well, if you really want to grow up and be spiritually complete, sell what you have and share it with those who need it. Then come and partner with Me."

This response stunned and saddened the prosperous young man. He just couldn't release his controlling grip, so he turned and walked away. (I guess he just didn't understand the deep reservoir of personal and spiritual wealth Jesus offered him.)

What happens next amazes me: Jesus watched him go. The young man disagreed with Jesus (and God!), yet Jesus did not run after him or try to force him to change his mind. He told the man the truth, honored his decision and allowed him to walk away.

Jesus left the responsibility for growth and change exactly where it belonged: with the young man. And we can follow Jesus' example. We need not control anyone else's reactions or decisions. Although we may need to tell our loved one the uncomfortable truth about their choices, it's not our responsibility to fix their mistakes, adjust their attitudes or alter their behavior. In fact, when we attempt to do that, it often backfires and we get an outcome we never wanted. Kay Grove, a grandmother and neighborhood Bible study leader, made the tough decision to release a relationship, and never regretted it:

For 12 years I struggled with how to be the perfect daughter-in-law to the perfect mother-in-law. I didn't feel like a perfectionist. I didn't want to be. I think life is too short to get hooked into trying so hard to be right all the time. Yet I wasn't sure how to deal with this personal relationship.

Then I heard a well-known speaker talk about getting along with the important people in your life. I remember where I was sitting at the Hershey Park Arena in Pennsylvania when he said, "Surrender the other person, yourself and your relationship to the Lord, or you may 'take on' some of the characteristics of the other person."

Right then, I made a decision. I wanted to be the "me" God created and not like someone else. I prayed for my mother-in-law, for me, and for our interactions. I gave it over to the Lord and released myself from trying to be what I could not anyway.

Things changed. Actually *I* changed. I couldn't fix anyone else, so I teamed with God to transform my own heart. There'll always be someone who has a nicer home than I have or is able to do things better than I do them. But it's okay. God is the only perfect one. And someday I'll share His perfection in heaven with Him. I find joy in that promise.

Off the Relational Roller Coaster

You know you're straining when you're overly discouraged by your failures.
JAN JOHNSON, *ENJOYING THE PRESENCE OF GOD*[5]

When we focus on trying to fix another person, it can seem like we're riding the world's steepest roller coaster. At first the ride might feel exhilarating. After all, we're living on the edge. But then after jolting ourselves up and down and around in circles (sometimes for years) with few straight stretches where we can catch a breath, we want off that carnival ride. We're tired and we hurt. (Even a good massage therapist couldn't rub out the stiff neck we got from the continuous whiplash.)

Author and counselor Pat Springle explains this relational roller-coaster ride as the Savior/Judas Complex.[6] He writes how our self-perceptions fluctuate, depending on whether the person we try to help is pleased or upset with us. When we operate in "savior mode," we see ourselves as worthwhile or indispensable. We're riding high. Then after our efforts to make everything right falter, we feel sad and inadequate. The other person expresses displeasure, and we feel unappreciated. We're riding low.

When we try to be a superwoman and fail (which is bound to happen no matter how talented, intelligent or spiritual we are), we can plunge into self-doubt and sometimes depression. The resulting unhealthy shame numbs us until we try to "help" again. The only way down from this relational roller coaster is to choose to press the stop lever: admit our humanness, God's compassionate sovereignty and the other person's dignity.[7]

God Makes All Things Right

Love comes when manipulation stops;
when you think more about the other person than about
his or her reactions to you. When you dare to reveal yourself fully.
When you dare to be vulnerable.

Dr. Joyce Brothers, well-known psychologist and author

Remember in the last chapter when I mentioned that tension-filled walk I took, begging God to remove my hurt and fix the problem between a friend and me? I sensed God asking me not to try to wiggle out of the pain, but to relax and trust Him because He was "doing something." I've been watching calmly (most of the time) and doing my best to follow His directions, and I think one thing He is doing is allowing me to experience what fixing and over-helping feels like to the help-*ee*.

It is often difficult for me to verbalize my feelings. Staying in my mind is easier for me than stating my emotions. But I've been thinking (see, I told you!) and I'm pretty sure that during the tensest time in that relationship, I felt smothered, misunderstood, not heard, inferior and quite frustrated. It seemed unfair to me. (Not fun! I don't wish that experience on anyone else.)

I wonder, *Have I unintentionally treated my husband this way at times?* I never realized it before, but I think I have. Ouch! Double ouch! I don't want to do this anymore. I think this is what God meant when He said to calm down and trust Him because He's "doing something." I believe God is showing me how it feels to experience both verbal and non-verbal fixing attempts—and I don't like it much. By the way, my friend and I have worked it through now and I realize she was concerned about me and trying to genuinely help, which ironically is exactly what I've wanted to do with my husband. Although this entire experience has been extremely uncomfortable for me, I do appreciate what God's teaching me. I'm seeing my husband through fresh eyes and feel a breath of fresh air flowing through our relationship. God is so good! As the psalmist wrote, "Everything he does is good and fair; . . . He sets his people free. . . . He is holy and wonderful" (Ps. 111:7,9, *NCV*).

How liberating to know that you and I don't have to perform God's job or fix His people. We can get off the relational roller coaster, grow quiet enough inside to gain our own insight, and joyfully trust God to work in the lives of those we care about.

Lord,
My desire is to treat others with respect and acceptance,
even when I don't agree with them and they don't agree with me.
I know I won't do this flawlessly. Only You are perfectly good and fair.
Please pour Your goodness and love through me to others.
I'm breathing lighter already.

CHAPTER 5

Will You Just Lighten Up?

"Who wants to take part in a sample coaching session?" asked our facilitator.

It was the first day of life coaches training.[1] None of us knew what to expect. I, the introvert, didn't wish to be the first to jump into the interactive teaching ring, yet I felt my hand slowly rise and saw the facilitator nod my way. Moving my chair to the front of the room, I faced the coach eyeball to eyeball. (*Gulp!*)

"What's up?" he asked. (He meant, "What do you want to be coached about?")

"I'd like to write another book for one of these publishers," I answered and rattled off a list of well-known Christian publishing houses. "But I'm not sure how to accomplish this."

In normal coaching style, he asked me "powerful questions" to help me discover optional solutions. I can't remember everything that transpired, but at the end of our discussion, he gave me a simple homework suggestion:

> Draw a circle on a piece of paper and print the word HARD inside. Make it look like a *Do Not Enter* traffic sign by marking a big slash through it. Next to this stop sign, write the word EASE. Do this before each coaching session or whenever you're feeling undue pressure to achieve.

"I'll do it," I said. (In coaching, optional responses to suggested assignments or challenges include saying *yes*, *no*, *I'll think about it* or offering a renegotiation.[2])

Hard   Ease

"That's not a very big assignment," shouted one of the participants. "Shouldn't she have a greater challenge?" (At the next workshop, *she* got the challenge she thought *I* needed. Her assignment? Make 20 cold sales calls within the next two days!)

"Joan tends to work too hard at everything she does," the facilitator responded. "This is enough challenge for her." He looked my way. "Is that true, Joan?" he asked.

"Yes," I said and grinned. *How did he know that? I've never met this guy before.*

Then in continued response to the woman's question, he said, "I heard the tension in Joan's voice—and noticed something else. Look at her hands now. See how they're open? During our entire discussion they were clenched into fists on her lap."

This coaching interchange happened 10 years ago and I've used adaptations of this stress-reducing technique ever since. This minute I'm looking at a 3-by-5 card with the crossed-out HARD sign on it. I read it to remind myself to *take it easy* while completing projects (like this book!). I also refer to it when reminding myself to lighten up and cease trying so hard to make my interactions and communications with others turn out just right. It helps me unclench my hands, heart and mind.

Adjusting Our Expectations

Sometimes we expect our relationships—at home, church or work—to be a constant support, unspoiled by conflicts, disappointments or imperfections. However, just like us, family members, friends and co-workers experience good *and* bad days (even years). Any of us can become bogged down in a personal muddle that renders us unavailable. Even those who love us deeply will not always meet our needs, understand our losses or flawlessly honor our gifts or values. And we won't for them, either.

These times can be upsetting and stressful, yet we can learn to breathe deeply, reduce silent (or verbal) panic, and flex. Although it will probably mean discovering and adjusting our misconceptions about how to get along with other people, we *can* grow and cultivate healthy and reasonable expectations for ourselves and our relationships.[3] Lauri Cruz, an RN, recalls how she began to adjust her expectations for herself:

> Several years ago while living in Chicago, two friends (a married couple) and I (single) started a group for 20-somethings that included both marrieds and singles. I'm a people-person, so it was exciting to watch everyone interact and have fun. As we grew and expanded our activities, I felt I was doing what God wanted me to do.
>
> "Lauri, we think it's time for the married couples to form our own group," my friends announced one day. Although surprised, I reluctantly agreed. My friends would lead the married group, while I would become the leader for the singles.
>
> *Okay . . . I can do this—with your help, Lord.* Soon I noticed the married group thrived while our singles group struggled to stay alive. I felt bummed yet determined. I didn't want to let anyone down, most of all God. After a year on my own, I invited a single friend to co-lead. We had some good months, yet much of the time it felt like "Lauri desperately trying to hold it all

together." I felt responsible for the group's success and was disappointed others didn't step up to help. *I can't let it fall apart. They need me.*

Then the co-leader and I had several disagreements, and he left. I lost my friend and it felt awful. The group dwindled and I became so frustrated that I made an appointment to talk with the associate pastor. I poured out my heart. He understood because he was the original youth pastor for these same singles and struggled to hold the group together, too. However, the group did expand greatly under his leadership.

"What am I going to do?" I asked.

"Lauri, look at your hands," he said. I did. "Are there any nail prints in them?"

"No," I admitted while staring at my upturned palms.

"Well, you're not Jesus then. *He* is perfect, not you. Go easy on yourself," he said. "It's not your job to save your friends. Neither is it their job to meet your needs. Only God can do that." I'll never forget his wise counsel.

He knew I enjoyed the Bible studies and suggested I write them down and send them to the singles group via email, instead of hitting my head against a wall trying to get the group together. I tried this and loved it. My ministry now stretches past the Chicago area and goes around the world. As a traveling nurse, I can email these devotionals from anywhere I live (now in California).

It's freeing for me. Because I'm imperfect (I admit it), that old "I must do it right, help everyone and disappoint no one" complex creeps up occasionally. But when it does, I just look at my hands.

It's Not So Hard

Most of us wish we could offer unconditional support and consistently significant help to those we care about. I know I do. But because I'm not omnipresent, omnipotent and omniscient, I can't. (Author Mary Pierce and I reached that conclusion in chapter 2, remember?)

Yet recently, my playing-God characteristics surfaced again when I felt guilty that I wasn't spending more time helping my daughter-in-law, Anne, with newborn baby, Sam, and his older brothers, Luke and Max. *If I were a better grandmother and mother-in-law, I'd figure out a way to help her so that she could rest or get away for a couple hours.* It didn't matter that we babysat the older boys while Anne and Sam were in the hospital or a week later watched the three boys while Rich and Anne went to dinner, or that we planned to care for our grandsons every other Thursday night while their parents attended small group at church. I wanted to do *more.* I recalled my sleepless nights and zombie days as a young mom and wanted to help relieve her stress.

I tried to fight off the guilt monsters with an inner "face up to reality" speech. *Joan, you love Anne and your grandchildren. Of course you'd like to help more, but you work full-time—speaking, training, coaching, writing and maintaining the Intentional Woman Network. You also have three granddaughters, a daughter and son-in-law, a husband, a house, friends, an extended family and health issues to address.*

Then it hit me: To help more, I'd have to be superwoman. (I'm not!) It's egotistical of me to even hint that I might be able to do it all. Still, I felt sad. So what could I do?

Tell Anne how I felt. (Duh!) One morning, I drove to her house, sat down and looked her in the eye. I shared what I wished to do but couldn't, how I loved her and felt guilty, suggested she and Rich ask when they needed support, and told her that Papa and I would help as we were able. *Now, Joan, was that so hard?*

"And now, Lord, thank you for giving me so many people, so many opportunities to love. But please forgive me when I fail them; help them to forgive me, and me to forgive myself. You made me human, and there is only so much of me to go around."

Marjorie Holmes, *Lord, Let Me Love*[4]

Although we long to provide *and* receive total support at all times in every situation, there is blessing in accepting that it isn't possible—or wise. For if we met all our family's and friends' needs and desires and they met ours, we might be tempted to leave God out of our lives. And *that* would be the genuine tragedy.

For Sue Wilbur, an administrator, wife and grandmother, admitting imperfection helped her deal with her depression and dissatisfaction:

The man I loved for 22 years died unexpectedly in 1997. Though not a perfect marriage, because of Jesus' powerful intervention and our commitment to sobriety, our last six years together brought joy and peace to us both. I had no regrets or words left unsaid when Jim died. Painfully, I began the life of a widow.

The possibility of remarrying never entered my mind. My first husband gave me two beautiful children and more than my share of bruises—physical, mental, verbal and emotional. We divorced. After Jim, my second husband, died, I decided a third marriage was not necessary since I had already experienced both a good and a bad one.

God must have a sense of humor, for two years and two months after Jim's death, I married Jerry, a man I had known nearly 30 years earlier. At age 50, I thought this relationship would be a breeze. *What more could I learn about family, marriage or relationships? After all, I have been the perfect wife twice, the perfect martyr and the perfect widow.*

Yet six years later I felt depressed, miserable and alone. I wished Jerry would have an affair so that I would have biblical grounds for divorce. I lived a lie. No one knew, not even those I worked with at church. I hid it from everyone but God.

During a women's retreat (that I planned!) at Zion National Park, our keynote speaker, Joan Webb, introduced the Wheel of Life and Roles Pinwheel exercises.[5] These tools helped me identify my current roles and measure my levels of satisfaction in each. They caused me to honestly reevaluate my life. I had to admit I was depressed and that my "perfect wife" role brought me practically no satisfaction.

This was God's wake-up call. Jerry had been nothing but patient during these six years, and I knew my dissatisfaction was not caused by him but by my need to be perfect and have an ideal relationship. As I did years earlier when leaving my alcohol addiction, I admitted my need for God's intervention as well as my responsibility to cooperate with Him. The week after the retreat, I made two appointments—one with my doctor and one with a counselor. I still see my counselor regularly and take an anti-depressant daily.

I know God's Word gives explicit guidelines for wives and relationships, but merely reading and studying is not enough for me. I need to *live* them—and I want to. God is the reason I've ceased obsessing about being perfect. God is the reason I now look at Jerry as a gift, rather than an intruder into my impossibly perfect world.

Can't Force Love

Every close relationship has known conflict and resolution—
or no closeness exists! Where love exists, there will be a willingness
to listen, to understand, to tolerate, to confront, to forgive, to compromise,
to resolve the distinctive "differences" we have.

CAROL KENT, SECRET LONGINGS OF THE HEART[6]

Healthy love resists trying to control how someone shows their concern or affection for us. Sometimes when attempting to fulfill our personal relational dreams, we push our ideas about "ideal" thoughtfulness and kindness on others. We may attempt to remove another's pain to reduce our discomfort. Or perhaps we fail to allow for individuality and squelch perceptions, thoughts or feelings that don't match our own. This type of "love" can be limiting and inhibit understanding, contentment and cooperation, whether in a marriage relationship, friendship, church or work partnership.

Elisabeth Elliot, author of *Love Has a Price Tag*, writes about her husband's observation about wives:

> If she is very generous, [she] may allow that her husband lives up to perhaps 80 percent of her expectations. There is always the other 20 percent that she would like to change, and she may chip away at it for the whole of their married life without reducing it by very much. She may, on the other hand, simply decide to enjoy the 80 percent, and both of them will be happy.[7]

Elliot's suggestion, though about marriage, can be applied to any important relationship. "Enjoying the 80 percent" does not mean we neglect to share our true needs, desires and hurts. Neither does it mean we accept physical, emotional, verbal or spiritual abuse. In marriage, we have a God-given responsibility to refuse to be treated this way.[8] "Enjoying the 80 percent" means that we cultivate a grace-filled heart—as Elisabeth Elliot writes, "let thanksgiving be the habit of your life."[9]

Genuine love accepts what the other person is able or willing to give at any given time. No matter what, our closest relationships and partnerships will eventually frustrate or disappoint us. Imperfect people living in a flawed world do not make perfect alliances, friendships, partnerships, marriages or families. They can make useful, loving, compassionate, encouraging partnerships and moments, but they will not be perfect all the time. To expect perfection is unrealistic, as Sandy Hank, a wife, mother and grandmother, found out:

> It was Christmas week and I sat in a hospital room with my seriously ill three-month-old daughter, Anne Marie. She refused to eat, had already lost weight, and continued to vomit. We heard faint music down the hall, but no carolers, clowns or visitors would come to cheer us up. We were quarantined.
>
> My two other children sat at home without their mom. It was four-year-old Mark's birthday and I couldn't plan his party, buy his gifts or finish getting ready for Christmas. I felt frustrated and sad—depressed and angry, too—for myself, for Anne, for the two kids left at home. This was not what I had planned. It wasn't fair.
>
> There were only two children in the infectious disease ward that night: my daughter and a special needs child who looked to be in very bad shape. The child's father stayed close to her side. After chatting intermittently throughout the afternoon, this tired father asked, "You have any other children?"

"Yes, a boy and a girl," I answered. "It's my son's birthday and I'm bummed that I'm not there to prepare. You have other children?"

"Yes," he replied. "We have another child with the same disability as this one."

I turned my head as tears formed in my eyes. Even though this was not the perfect dream I had for Anne Marie's first Christmas, she was being treated and she would recover. My other children were healthy and well-cared for. I caught my breath as God seemed to whisper in my ear, "Sandy, this is My gift to you: *a new perspective*. Life isn't totally black or white, all good or all bad. Every holiday, birthday or life experience won't always be just *so*. Some things will disappoint, but you have a choice about how to 'see' it. And I sense your grateful heart right now. Merry Christmas."

Jesus' Imperfect Reality

We can count our blessings, or we can count calamities.
BARBARA JOHNSON[10]

Even the King of kings wasn't born into a perfect situation, community or family. Ken Gire, author of *Intimate Moments with the Savior*, writes, "And so, with barely a ripple of notice, God stepped into the warm lake of humanity. Without protocol and without pretension. . . . Yes, there were angels announcing the Savior's arrival—but only to a band of blue-collar shepherds. And yes, a magnificent star shone in the sky to mark his birthplace—but only [a few] foreigners bothered to look up and follow it."[11]

It's likely that teenage Mary's friends shunned her for being pregnant before she and Joseph lived together as husband and wife. *It wasn't fair. They didn't understand.* By government order,

Mary had to leave her family just when she needed them most. *It wasn't right.* Joseph had few supplies and a full-term pregnant wife to care for on that long uncomfortable journey to Bethlehem. *Didn't anyone care?* Once they arrived, they found no decent place to stay. *What's good about that?*

Yet God delivered His perfect Son anyway, on a scratchy patch of straw. Jesus agreed to leave His Father's side to live with us in imperfection so that we could have the opportunity to reconnect with a perfect God. As Richard Peace, author of *Learning to Love Ourselves*, reminds us, "He took upon his perfect self the imperfection of all of us."[12] He is not surprised by our limitations or repulsed by our messiness. He understands— and He redeems. With Jesus as our example, we can stop the silent demand that imperfection go away. We can unclench our hearts and enjoy one another. He gives us imperfect joy now and the hope of flawless delight later. Now that's a relief!

Lord,
my relationships will never be perfect.
As paradoxical as it seems,
I know admitting this
is the way to a more peaceful and fulfilling life.

Relief Reminder

Before reading the next section, "The Relief of Imperfect Emotions, Minds and Bodies," take a break and play (not *work*!) through the Relief Guide for Imperfect Relationships and Families. Do it alone or invite someone to join you.

The Relief of Imperfect Relationships and Families

After reading chapters 4 and 5, take some time to respond to the following questions and exercises in your Relief Journal.

1. Which story, anecdote or illustration in chapters 4 and 5 resonated with you most? In what way?

2. Name a time you felt respected, listened to or valued by another person. What did he or she do or not do?

3. Read Matthew 19:16-22. What do you learn from Jesus in His interaction with the affluent young man? How can you apply Jesus' example to your own life?

4. List the relationships in your life (it doesn't need to be an exhaustive list). Put an *X* beside the name(s) of anyone you feel has ever attempted to change or fix you. Circle the names of those you have ever wanted to change or fix. What do you notice about your list? How much overlap is there between the *X*ed and the circled names?

5. Describe the joy of *not* fixing someone else, and spend several minutes contemplating where that joy comes from.

6. Read the following verses:

Be humble and gentle. Be patient with each other, making allowance for each other's faults because of your love. Always keep yourselves united in the Holy Spirit, and bind yourselves together with peace (Eph. 4:2-3, *NLT*).

Learn from me, for I am gentle and humble in heart (Matt. 11:29).

Take a few moments to reflect on these passages and talk with God about what you're learning, sensing and/or feeling right now. Then jot down your prayer in your journal and date it.

Lord,
help me to be as gentle and respectful with myself and others
as You are with me.

Optional: The Listening Game

It is impossible to over-emphasize the immense need [people] have
to be really listened to, to be taken seriously, to be understood.
PAUL TOURNIER, *TO UNDERSTAND EACH OTHER*[1]

Listening to another person is an excellent way to show gentleness and respect (see 1 Pet. 3:15). For a fun yet meaningful exercise, play the Listening Game with a partner. If you're reading this book on your own, ask a friend to play with you. If you're playing through the Relief Guides in a group setting, pair up one-on-one.

1. One woman shares her response to questions 1, 2 or 4 above. The other woman listens without any interruptions for 2 to 3 minutes. She offers no advice,

consultation, Scripture verses or "I did that, too!" comments. She may wish to make eye contact, smile or lean forward, but no words.

2. Switch roles so that the first listener can share her responses to question 1, 2 or 4 above while the other woman listens without any interruptions or words.

3. After both have talked and listened, discuss how it felt to be the talker and the listener. What was it like to talk without being interrupted? What was it like to listen without saying anything?

Listening is a win-win for relationships. Gary Collins, PhD, a Christian life coach, writes, "Sometimes people get new insights when they stop long enough to talk about their lives with someone who is willing to listen."[2] But listening helps not only the one being listened to, but it also lowers the listener's urgency to appear knowledgeable and wise or to fix the situation or behavior. Although listening without commenting—or talking without being interrupted—may feel uncomfortable at first (because it is generally an unfamiliar way to relate) after a little practice, it offers loads of relief—to *everyone*.

The Relief of
Imperfect Emotions,
Minds and Bodies

CHAPTER 6

Never Underestimate the Power of a Nervous Breakdown

*Some feelings are more comfortable than others,
but they all send us messages
we couldn't live without—about danger, pleasure,
loss, comfort, excess. . . .
Our bodies will react and respond to the
heat of our passions even when we think
we're being totally cool.*

Enid Howarth and Jan Tras, *The Joy of Imperfection*[1]

Several years ago after experiencing repeated bouts of heart palpitations and rapid pulse rate (I called it "my clunking heart"), the doctor sent me to a physical therapist.[2] The goal? To teach me methods for alleviating stress-induced symptoms.

The therapist suggested I try biofeedback to help me learn to relax more effectively. He attached me to a device, showed me how to monitor my responses, and then left the room. Immediately my pulse quickened and my mind tightened (although I tried hard to make certain that wouldn't happen!).

Within minutes, the meter's arrow flipped wildly and then disappeared off the dial. "Somebody's fiddling with the controls from the other room," I surmised. "Cut it out! Quit messin' with my mind!" I wanted out of there!

When the doctor returned, he calmly said, "I guess we'll just forget using this again."

I thought I broke the machine. Well, maybe I did—sometimes I have a difficult time relaxing. (Hey, I forget to breathe!) Today while chuckling and shaking my head over this past experience, I'm reminded how intricately you and I are created. The mind affects the emotions (and vice versa). Emotions affect the body. What happens in the body effects the soul (which is your personality) and actions. Maybe it's not always in that order.

My point is this: It's all so exquisitely intertwined. And that's exactly how God planned it and the way He works in us:

> If we have the idea that there is no connection between the natural (our temperament and personality structure) and the supernatural (our spiritual lives), we are seriously mistaken. Both our feelings and our faith operate through the same personality equipment. . . . [God] doesn't drill a hole in the tops of our skulls and with some magical, mystical funnel pour His grace into us.[3]

"To truly love God with all our heart, soul, mind, and strength (Mark 12:30) requires that we know not only God but also our interior—the nature of our own heart, soul, and mind," writes Peter Scazzero.[4] Our loving Creator didn't plan for you to compartmentalize yourself or grade one part better than another. Everything counts. Mind, body, emotions, soul and, yes, *spirit*—the part of you that connects with the Spirit of the all-powerful and loving God as He confirms that you are His daughter.

It's a Head-spinning Deal!

The Spirit himself testifies with our spirit that we are God's children.
ROMANS 8:16

Look, can we talk? (Well, you know what I mean.) I've been writing this book for months now, and I've waited until the last moment to address "The Relief of Imperfect Emotions, Minds and Bodies." What's up with that?

[Brooke] Shields has no regrets about going public [with her depression]: "It's made me responsible to it. I might have wanted to sweep it under the rug and pretend it didn't happen."[5]

I believe this topic is *huge*—and honestly, it intimidates me. I think it's such a big deal because of my interactions with women through the years (and I've been around awhile!) who include friends, relatives and acquaintances; coaching and life plan clients; women in corporate, casual and church settings; women at Bible studies, workshops and conferences whether in my town or across the continents; and my observations of women in television, movies, politics and the news. I can't think of one woman I've known or read about who has not been affected by this area of imperfect emotions, minds and bodies. Under this subject's lid simmers a stew of sub-issues including body image, dieting, exercise, nutrition, hormone treatment, disabilities, anorexia, bulimia, overeating, PMS, peri-menopause, menopause, post-partum problems, depression, worry, denial, malaise, inferiority, false and real guilt, addictions, mental illness, grief, loss, aging, abuse, codependency, counseling, physical therapy and other publicized problems and possible solutions. (You get the picture?)

It makes my head spin just re-reading that paragraph, but that's not the only reason I've stalled writing these two chapters. The topic is deeply personal and I don't know whether to admit that truth or ignore it on these pages. In fact, I'm sitting just staring at the computer screen right now.

You Perfect Yet?

As far back as I can remember, I was teased about being *too perfect*. As a kid, my brother nicknamed me "Perfecto" and my beloved mother said I acted "like a martyr." For some reason, people looked at me and assumed, "Joan has no problems, disabilities, quirks or hang-ups. Look at her perfect circumstances, opportunities and relationships." Many times I sensed pressure to keep up that image and not rock the boat.

But I *have* swayed the ship. The truth's out! Perfecto and her emotions, mind and body are flawed. I've faced PMS, prolonged peri-menopause and menopausal problems, depression, burnout, codependency, spousal obsession, fibromyalgia, body image issues, weight loss gone haywire, sleep deprivation, counseling, antidepressants withdrawal, an anorexic teenage daughter, and the homelessness and multiple addictions of loved ones in my extended family. Within the last year, the medical community finally heard me (and my husband, who had been saying it for years) and diagnosed me with severe sleep apnea. (Doctors kept saying I looked too good to have that problem!) I now use a CPAP machine at night and rarely fall asleep at my desk, in the car or at other inappropriate times anymore.[6]

All this merely illustrates that I'm like everyone else— touched by a flawed reality—and admittedly humbled by my imperfect emotions, mind and body.

After my burnout pushed me to a near nervous breakdown, I finally went to a counselor. I told him emphatically, "I am not crazy! I'm not perfect, either. I'm a regular person." The truth is, all of us regular people are human and flawed. We need a Savior. And there's the good news: We have one.

Have some of you noticed that we are not yet perfect? (No great surprise, right?) . . . I tried keeping rules and working my head off to please God, and it didn't work. So I quit being a "law man" so that I could be God's man. Christ's life showed me how, and enabled me to do it. I identified myself completely with him (Gal. 2:17,19-20, *THE MESSAGE*).

Yesterday I received a smile-inspiring email from my daughter (who has recovered from her agonizing teenage anorexic years and is the lovely mother of three adorable little girls—yes, I know these are the words of a proud grandma!). "Mom, you asked what was so good about my week," she wrote. "Through several experiences God has personally assured me that He delights in me and my faltering baby steps to grow and serve Him. When I had given nothing to Him, He still loved and redeemed me. As I really grasp that Christ already paid for each of my sins and needs, I no longer feel like giving up. I don't need to be overwhelmed when I fail, because God isn't. He knew about it in advance and provided His Son to pay for it so that I can walk in grateful, ordinary obedience."

Like the many women who've shared inspiring stories in this book, I'm so glad God chooses to partner with imperfect women (and men, too!). He's not shocked by our human imperfections or sins (and there is a difference). God never means for us to remain in our dysfunction, denial and pain. As He did for Debbie Matlock, a library aide and single mother of two grown children, He'll reach deep into your ache and confusion, offering relief and inner healing:

Journal entry from August 10, several years ago:

> How much longer? Will I never locate the exit?
> I can't take much more. Please, someone, help me.
> My lifeblood drains away. How did I get here?
> I hate it! I want out. Get me out!

Journal entry from September 7 several years ago:

> I can't find it. Where is it? Oh, my! There is it—
> or the remains of it—at my feet. That faithful
> stone mask, ground almost to powder. What will
> I do? It kept me going. Each fear, hurt, injustice
> added another layer and made it stronger. It was
> unbreakable, impermeable until that final verbal
> blow and it crashed to the ground. What now?

Current journal entry:

> After my grandfather's death and a long, hard,
> unhealthy marriage, I ended up traveling to places
> I never imagined I'd go. Darkness. Depression.
> Despair. I waited for death to overtake me. Upon
> landing in a mental hospital, I saw the relation-
> ships, responsibilities and gifts that once brought
> me pride scattered useless around my feet.

With my self-made supports stripped away, God became real. The Bible, once mere words, spoke directly to me. A year into recovery, I read Haggai 2:3-9: "Who saw this house in its former glory? . . . Be strong, for I am with you . . . Don't fear . . . This present house will be greater than the former . . . I'll grant you peace."

Peace. *Ah.* Inner peace. That's I wanted. *Lord, could this new house mean You'll make a new me, better than before my breakdown?* "Oh yes, Deb," God assured. "Don't fret. I have a plan. You'll return much better than before."

Never underestimate the transforming power of a nervous breakdown. I can now laugh and sometimes joke about my stay in the mental hospital and the five-year struggle out of depression. In my pain I learned to trust.

And now? I have a new peace-filled life. I'm alive as I never dreamed possible. In high school, I worked in the library and loved it. Now in my late 40s, after raising my children, facing singleness and supporting myself, I applied for and landed a position with one of the best public library systems in the country.

The clincher? Every morning on my drive to work, I pass the psychiatric facility where I once resided and "died." Just as God promised, a better life, a "new house" came forth from the ashes of depression and death. Astounding how God works, huh? Not a day passes that I don't thank Him. Yes, God can bring good out of a nervous breakdown!

Accepting Your Feelings

Each man's life is but a breath.
Man is a mere phantom as he goes to and fro;
He bustles about, but only in vain . . .
But now Lord, what do I look for? My hope is in you.
PSALM 39:5-7

Perhaps you believe that you must put on a happy mask so that others will think you are a strong, spiritual person. Even when you are hurt or depressed, you smile and attempt to prove to your world that all is right. Perhaps as a child, your role models gave you the impression that it was inconvenient, cowardly or ungodly to admit to disappointment, sadness, discouragement or anger. But what you learned is a misconception. Although there is nothing wrong with maintaining a positive outlook (actually, it's a worthwhile approach to life), you need not pretend you never hurt.

"The Scriptures are much more realistic and kind to us than some Christians are, as they clearly show that it is possible for Christians to be very depressed," writes Dr. David Seamands in the book *Healing for Damaged Emotions*. "Before a person can deal with depression, he must acknowledge it."[7] Dr. Seamands contends that depression is not automatically a sign of spiritual failure; it can be an emotional comedown after spiritual victory. "Depression seems to be nature's emotional kickback," writes Seamands.[8]

Many nations looked up to King David, but he made major mistakes. He sinned. He experienced the rejection of trusted co-workers. He felt angry, jealous and hurt. Yet David was a truthful man who allowed himself to think, feel and be. Often in his psalms he expressed sadness, discouragement and confusion. His acceptance of reality and the resulting feelings of disappointment and pain led him again and again to God. And God called him "a man after his own heart" (see 1 Sam. 13:14 and Acts 13:22). Sometimes we feel happy, sometimes we feel sad, hurt, disappointed or angry. God never rejects us because we *feel*.

"Honesty before God requires the most fundamental risk of faith we can take: the risk that God is good, that God does love us unconditionally. It is in taking this risk that we discover our dignity."

Gerald G. May, MD, *Addiction and Grace*[9]

Maybe some of you have the impression that you *must* release your emotions or you'll burst. Instead of looking for the honest expression of your feelings, you let fly with bursts of rage, caustic sarcasm or whining self-pity (to name a few). You may find it difficult to understand how another woman might choose to hide her emotions behind a grin. But your explosive display of emotions may get you in just as much trouble as the woman who pretends or isolates. The truth is, *God loves both of you*. I mean, He *really* cares about you. He's made provision for you to live in harmony with your emotions and thoughts. So please take care of yourself. Grab whatever courage you can find and get the help you need, regardless of how uncomfortable it makes you—or others—feel. Call a doctor. Ask questions. Share with a compassionate listener. Your spouse. An empathetic friend. A transparent ministry leader. See a competent counselor—and if you don't connect with the first one you visit, try another. Just start the process.

Taking Care of Yourself

One of the assets of being human
is having the option of changing whatever situation presents itself. . . .
If the grass on the other side is greener, maybe your own needs fertilizer.
PAUL L. WARNER, *FEELING GOOD ABOUT FEELING BAD*[10]

There was a plot to get rid of Jesus (see Matt. 12:14-15). He knew it and left the place of danger. He didn't stop living His God-given purpose, but He took responsibility for His own safety at the time. Later, when the moment was right, Jesus died on the cross. But at this particular time, He removed himself from jeopardy.

You can take responsibility for yourself, your own emotions, thoughts and health. You don't need to stay in a personal state that is detrimental to you (either internally or externally).

You do have the option to get help or even leave for a while. Jesus did.[11]

Perhaps by "sticking it out" you think you demonstrate spiritual tenacity or moral character. That may be true; it may be that you need to stay, confront the issues and make your own changes. Just remember: You can't change anyone else, only yourself. No doubt about it, self-care is modeled by Jesus and acceptable with God. Isn't that a relief?

Above All Else

For years I read Proverbs 4:23 and thought it was a nice sentiment written by a wise man.[12] "Above all else, guard your heart, for it is the wellspring of life" (Prov. 4:23). Then one day I saw these words with new eyes. Drawn to research the Hebrew meaning of each word, I paraphrased the verse based on my findings. As a result, I no longer doubt the validity or the godliness of self-care. How about you?

Proverbs 4:23
First and foremost—above all else—
your greatest responsibility, priority and honor
is to protect, maintain, guard, preserve and
nurture your soul.
Your soul, the real you, makes up your unique self
with your mind, feeling, will and personality.
So guard your inner self, for out of *it*
(not the external manifestations of
accomplishment, success,
failure, performance, money or appearance)
springs forth Life—your entire life,
everything you are.

CHAPTER 7

The Invisible Woman Comes Out of Hiding— Flaws and All

*Give your bodies to God. Let them be a living
sacrifice, holy—the kind he can accept.
When you think of what he has done for you,
is this too much to ask?
Don't copy the behavior and customs of this world,
but be a new and different person with a fresh
newness in all you do and think.
Then you will learn from your own experience
how his ways will really satisfy you.*

Romans 12:1-2, *TLB*

Endeavoring to practice what I teach, I took off on an intentional self-care morning get-away. My plan? Take a walk to a
nearby restaurant for a protein-packed breakfast, leisurely read
the paper (one of my personal enjoyments, but I know it isn't
for everyone!), walk to the pool area, do stretches in the
warmth of the whirlpool and water exercises in the lap pool.
Then relax in the shade for a while before going back to work.

Everything proceeded according to plan. Before heading to
the whirlpool, I stopped to use the restroom so that I wouldn't

have to do it later in the middle of my aqua-aerobics workout. (Thus avoiding the wet swimsuit dance; I never can get it adjusted and hooked correctly when it's soggy!) I covered the toilet seat with toilet paper as my mother told me to do when a kid. Duties completed, I headed for the pool.

I set my towel and sun screen on the last empty lounge chair. European vacationers occupied the other chairs (their lovely accents gave them away, but I'd already noticed the tour bus parked on the street). Peeling off the color-coordinated sweat suit I wore over my swim wear, I discovered wads of toilet paper hanging from the back of my bathing suit. So much for the perfect plan and the "together" image I hoped to portray! Imperfection sneaks up on me again, just when I think I've done everything possible to keep it at bay!

Sneaking Up on You

Today eating humble pie will be a piece of cake.
ENID HOWARTH AND JAN TRAS, *DAILY IMPERFECTIONS*[1]

Speaking of "sneaking up" on you . . . If you're older than 25, you've probably experienced this sneaky aging thing. (On my twenty-sixth birthday I confided to my hair stylist, "I'm on the downhill slide toward 30." Thirty seemed so old to me! Little did I know back then.)

A laugh line here, a gray hair there and a flabby muscle over there. Then a hint of cellulite—it starts slowly and spreads. Before you know it, the waist expands, you can't see the fine print on the aspirin bottle and premature menopausal sleeplessness threatens.

If you're between the ages of 12 and 25, you're feeling the pressure, too. Maybe no gray hair (yet), but you see skinny models and perfectly air-brushed celebrities selling everything from clothes to bank loans, motorcycles, snacks and prescription drugs—and secretly wish you looked like one of them. The inevitable padding that arrives with puberty feels troublesome (and cumbersome) when compared to the media's ideal woman. Author Debra M. Cooper, in her novel *Behind the Broken Image*, writes of a "system that endeavors to shape young girls into something instead of someone."[2] In her book *Soul Hunger*, Sandy Richardson writes that "even women who don't have an eating disorder tend to equate self-esteem with dress size. We live in a society that values thinness in women above nearly every other attribute."[3]

"The [links between stress and aging] emphasize the importance of managing life stress, to take it seriously if one feels stressed, to give your body a break, and make life changes that promote well-being."

Elissa Epel, psychiatrist at the University of California, San Francisco[4]

It's likely that no matter what your age, you're a little (or a lot) dissatisfied with some part of your body. Your eyes (wrong color? straight eyelashes?), hair (too curly? limp?), thighs (they've bonded and you wish they weren't so close!). Your best friend has a cute, curvy derrière, but yours is too flat? Funny thing, she likes yours! Maybe you think your neck is too long or too short. Maybe you're actually pleased with how you look, except for one small issue and you can't stop focusing on it. I probably missed your unique body-part pet peeve, but I'll stop. If I listed every possible complaint, I'd fill the entire chapter.

There is an epidemic of body dissatisfaction in our homes, communities, schools, churches, country and the world. Why else would nearly every magazine on the newsstand flash numerous feature articles pertaining to diets, exercise, eating disorders, plastic surgery, makeovers and fashion camouflaging—in *every* issue?

Just when I thought I couldn't stomach another how-to-look-like-a-model article, I noticed a title that intrigued me: "I Am Not My Body!" *I am not my body*. We know somewhere down deep that it's true, but as the media swamps us with images of perfect bodies we can never have, we become persuaded we *are* our bodies. Author Lisa Sandin, whose left arm is a short stub with a small hand and three fingers, writes how she was taught as a child "that bodies come in all shapes, colors and sizes and that everyone struggles in some way with the inadequacies of their bodies." Later in her essay she discloses, "In my alternately formed body, I have learned patience, determination, frustration and success. . . . I am not my body. I am my words, my ideas and my actions. I am filled with love, humor, ambition and intelligence. I am a creative spirit, a fellow human walking the planet, who just like you, is so much more than my body."[5] By the time I finished reading Sandin's powerful thoughts, I felt relieved—like I'm good enough as I am, without trying to do yet another thing to obtain a perfect-looking body.

My friend Grayce Gusmano—a marriage-family therapist, an eating-disorders counselor and an Intentional Woman presenter—has had hundreds of encounters with women who feel society's pressure to appear perfect. While chatting with Grayce recently, she noted how Mae West, the bosomy, blonde-bombshell actress and sex symbol of the early twentieth-century, reminded her of women today. West once said, "I used to be Snow White, but I drifted."

Grayce said, "In my work with women, I see them drift from a sense of wonder at their own uniqueness. They give away their personal, womanly power to a relationship and/or culture that enslaves them and prods them to reach the ideal size, weight or career position. And in the end they are profoundly dissatisfied, because they can't reach perfection. Many of these women never saw their unique worth mirrored back to them because they experienced previous painful and traumatic events. They never awakened to the truth of their individual worth. Recovery for these women includes reclaiming their God-given power to define themselves in ways that accept and celebrate their unique bodies, temperaments, talents and capabilities."[6]

Search for Body Perfectdom

Eating disorders can be silent killers that too often go unnoticed.
LYNN GREFE, CEO OF THE NATIONAL EATING DISORDERS ASSOCIATION[7]

Sometimes the quest for "body perfectdom" leads to an eating disorder such as anorexia, bulimia or EDNOS (Eating Disorder Not Otherwise Specified).[8] Although accurate statistics about these secret-driven eating disorders remain difficult to obtain, records indicate that up to 10 million women and girls suffer the confusing (and sometimes life-threatening) results of anorexia and bulimia, and an additional 25 million suffer from EDNOS.[9] These statistics cover only the United States of America. My mind boggles when attempting to fathom the worldwide affects of this growing problem. In a book about the relief of imperfection, I cannot keep silent about this joy-robbing practice of many lovely women—Christians included—women like Jen Smith, a ministry volunteer and small-business owner:

> I was thin, but not thin enough. Size two wouldn't do. I wanted to be the thinnest person I knew. As a hair stylist, I constantly worked in front of a mirror. That proved dangerous for me, because I ruthlessly compared myself to the women in my chair.

Growing up, I used food for comfort. When I developed anorexia in my early 20s, I believed I needed to rob myself of that comfort because I felt so unworthy. I punished myself if my stomach growled. As I continued to lose weight, I grew crabby and blamed my husband. *If he'd just spend more time with me, I'd feel better.* Yet I didn't make that idea much fun! Perhaps I wanted him to feel as bad inside as I did. *If he loved me enough, I'd at least like myself a little.* My emaciated brain really got mixed-up!

The pain of my eating disorder coupled with our infertility threw me into deep depression. Every time I saw a baby in the grocery store or sat behind a family at church, I sobbed. After battling anorexia for seven years, I eventually realized (after a few eye-opening experiences and talking with caring experts) that no one else cared if I wore a size zero. I'm the only one who wanted me to be that thin. I realized it was my own responsibility to get well and no one could do it for me. I went to the doctor and got an anti-anxiety anti-depressant. It helped. I was finally being responsible for my own health.

Changing proved to be a huge challenge—anorexia was my identity. I learned God isn't the grand magician I believed He was. Out of love for me, He doesn't just point His finger and grant whatever I think I need. That wouldn't benefit me. I realize growth is *my* responsibility and privilege, although it's quite difficult at times.

I can be a clean freak, yet that's changing, too. I know that when mail on the table or shoes at the front door bother me too much, its because I feel flawed for some reason and don't want the house to look as messy as I feel. I'm a different person now, one my husband wants to be around. Seeing myself through Christ's eyes makes all the difference! He believes in me.

I'm enough for God just as I am, so I'm learning to be enough for myself, as well. I work in my hair styling business again. Amazingly, God brings me clients experiencing depression, infertility and eating disorders. He's allowing my story to bring Him glory and help others. I'm smiling here. Once I felt so empty, but now my life feels full.

Example Is the Greatest Gift

Don't lord it over the people assigned to your care,
but lead them by your good example.
1 PETER 5:3, *NLT*

As I mentioned in the last chapter, one reason this section feels so challenging for me to write is because it's personal and I'm torn about how much to share. The other night I asked my daughter if I could write the following story. She said yes.

After high school, Lynnette chose to delay college for a year and live at home to work and pursue acting opportunities in the Minneapolis-St. Paul area. Because she graduated with honors, her teachers thought that wasn't the perfect choice, but Richard and I respected Lynnette's decision and trusted that she'd resume her studies when it felt right. Her commitment to education never wavered, so during that year we researched colleges and universities. Several times we visited Northwestern College in Orange City, Iowa, and discovered it offered her a theater scholarship and the ability to design her own "exercise science" major. (She graduated four years later and met her husband there.)

While driving home from a preparatory visit to NWC, we stopped to eat at a small-town restaurant along the route. Sitting across from one another in a narrow booth, our conversation turned serious as I shared about my recovery from burnout, work addiction, perfectionism and codependency, although I'm not certain we knew all those labels yet. I think I shared how terrifying it was for me to change the way I related to her father—she had watched my kowtowing behavior through the years. I shared that I thought I was showing love by biting my tongue, stuffing down my feelings and trying to make everything just right.

I wondered if my unhealthy patterns contributed to Lynnette's eating disorder. During her intense anorexic times, I had sometimes suggested she share her pain with her dad, but she couldn't and didn't. How sadly ironic that I wanted her to do what I couldn't do myself!

Lord, hear my prayer! . . .
Don't turn away from me in this time of my distress . . .
My health is broken, and my heart is sick . . .
My food is tasteless, and I have lost my appetite.
I am reduced to skin and bones because of all my
groaning and despair . . .
I lie awake, lonely as a solitary sparrow on the roof.
But you yourself never grow old.
You are forever, and your years never end.

Psalm 102:1-7, *TLB*

Lynnette witnessed the results of my decision to slow down, practice saying no to others' unrealistic requests, leave my business, get counseling and change the way I related to Richard—all new behavior for me. When I went away by myself to try to find Joan again, I asked Richard to talk with the kids about it all. He lovingly gathered both Lynnette and her brother, Rich, and said, "Your mom is really hurting right now. We need to try to be understanding and help as we can." Together they worked on updating my home office for my eventual homecoming. Each evening at 5:45 she watched as Richard rested on the living room sofa and waited for my prearranged 6:00 P.M. phone call—my one link to reality back home. His concern touched her soul.

"Mom, you saved my life, you know," Lynnette said as we munched on dinner that night, on the way home from North-western.

With tears in my eyes, I stared at her. I didn't know what to say. I think I finally asked, "What do you mean?"

"Well, I saw that it *is* possible to change. I watched you and knew I could do it, too—that it wouldn't be impossibly hard. Your courage gave me courage. I realized it was *my* responsibility to be healthy again. I could do it." Lynnette's life-threatening anorexia lasted less than a year. The residual mental and emotional fallout hung on for several more.

Helping my children wasn't the primary reason I changed. I admit that while in the throes of burnout, I felt heartsick because I sensed I hadn't raised Rich and Lynnette as I'd planned. Yet by the time I reached bottom and started the long uphill process to health, I didn't do it for them. I did it for me—to obey God's prompting to take responsibility for my own needs, sin, growth and recovery.

This level of self-care is precisely what we are told to do in Scripture: "Don't compare yourself with others. Each of you must take responsibility for doing the creative best you can with your own life" (Gal. 6:3, *THE MESSAGE*). The most beneficial thing we can do for our children, colleagues, friends and loved ones is deal honestly with our own impossible pursuit of perfection (to be God-like), our resentment and self-image problems, anxiety difficulties, unhealthy relationships, damaging obses-

sions, and lack of faith. God graciously gives us the responsibility and privilege to develop our own spiritual, mental and emotional muscles and make positive changes. Acknowledging our
need is not easy. It's painful to risk revealing our secrets, so we
often turn our energy away from dealing with our own growth
and concentrate instead on controlling or fixing others. (As I
did when I tried to get Lynnette to change, but wouldn't myself.)

In a rare unmasked moment, a talented, strong-willed and
deeply caring mother commented to me, "I see the pained way
my children and others relate to me. I guess I need help. But I'm
not going to get it. Changing now would hurt too many people."
This dedicated Christian woman failed to realize that she could
favorably influence her family and friends by confronting her
own perfectionistic attitudes and behavior and committing to
personal change and growth. We can offer others a superior gift:
a healthy example. And it's never too late, as Donna Baldwin, a
retired administrative assistant and grandmother shares:

Journal entry, August 1969:

> Today I took back my given name: *Donna*. For
> years, everyone called me Debbie after actress
> Debbie Reynolds. I never liked the name Donna
> because it reminded me of my childhood pain
> (alcoholic parents, abandonment, neglect, mis-
> treatment by stepdads and other relatives). All
> these years I've pushed down the pain. Maybe
> taking back my name will be a small step
> toward accepting my feelings and experiences
> and healing the awful shame. I know God's
> drawing me close, but it's foreign and uncom-
> fortable to feel comfort and love. I don't know
> how. I wish I did.

Journal entry, January 2005:

> I'm tired of the depression, bitterness, self-pity,
> confusion and this judgmental attitude.
> I couldn't fix me then and I can't fix me now.
> I want relief and fullness. Hopefully the honest
> release of my feelings—even all these years later—
> will prove beneficial. But I still don't quite know
> how. All I can do now is let it go and let it be
> God's to deal with.

Journal entry, December 2006:

> The other day I shared an ugly abuse memory
> with a counselor. I've never told anyone about
> that scary moment for my little sister and me
> when I was four years old. I always thought, *It's
> over and done*. But when Laura asked if she could
> pray for me, I said yes. To my surprise, I cried.
> Broken-hearted tears for something that hap-
> pened more than 60 years ago. I sobbed out the
> sorrow that robbed me of trust and burdened
> me with responsibility way too heavy to carry.
> A huge internal dam gave way and a wounded
> part of my life is mending. Now I know: It's
> never too late to face the pain and move toward
> emotional healing.

Coming to God with expectancy and faith will help us
understand His love, experience self-worth and know the joy
and freedom of transformation. God asks us to come out of
hiding, risk revealing our pain and flaws, and trust Him for the
future. In imperfect release, we find satisfaction and relief.

Relief Reminder

Before reading the next section, "The Relief of Imperfect Life-Work and Service," take a break and play through the Relief Guide for Imperfect Emotions, Minds and Bodies. Do it alone or invite someone to join you.

The Relief of Imperfect Emotions, Minds and Bodies

After reading chapters 6 and 7, I invite you to respond to the following questions and exercises in your Relief Journal. Remember that you always have the option to respond *Yes, No, Renegotiate* or *Later*. (See "Read This First!" for more explanation about these options.)

1. Which story or illustration amused, agitated or amazed you in chapters 6 and 7? In what way? I suggest you write your response in your journal and/or share with a caring friend.

2. What do you think about this idea of a body-dissatisfaction epidemic? What have you noticed? How has it affected you?

3. Acknowledging your fun and not-so-fun feelings is a positive step toward accepting and taking care of yourself. Skim the list on page 127 and check several words that describe how you're feeling today. If you're comfortable doing so, share your feelings with a friend or partner. As you take turns sharing, practice the Listening Game from the last Relief Guide. (Remember: No fixing someone else's feelings)! ☺

4. What affect does it have on your emotional, mental or physical life that Jesus paid for your sin and unbelief?

❏ absent-minded	❏ forgiven	❏ misunderstood	❏ sabotaged
❏ accepted	❏ frustrated	❏ mixed up	❏ saved
❏ afraid	❏ funny	❏ moody	❏ self-conscious
❏ agitated	❏ furious	❏ motivated	❏ self-destructive
❏ alone	❏ generous	❏ naive	❏ sinful
❏ appreciative	❏ gentle	❏ needy	❏ special
❏ aware	❏ grieving	❏ neglected	❏ squashed
❏ belittled	❏ grateful	❏ nervous	❏ stressed
❏ betrayed	❏ guarded	❏ numb	❏ strong
❏ bold	❏ healthy	❏ odd	❏ supported
❏ bummed	❏ heartbroken	❏ offended	❏ suspicious
❏ burned-out	❏ helpless	❏ old	❏ tearful
❏ calm	❏ hurt	❏ optimistic	❏ thankful
❏ caring	❏ impatient	❏ out of control	❏ thoughtful
❏ clueless	❏ imperfect	❏ overloaded	❏ torn
❏ committed	❏ inadequate	❏ overwhelmed	❏ troubled
❏ cranky	❏ indecisive	❏ overworked	❏ ugly
❏ crazy	❏ indifferent	❏ paralyzed	❏ unaccepted
❏ curious	❏ innovative	❏ patient	❏ uncomfortable
❏ deceived	❏ inquisitive	❏ peeved	❏ uplifted
❏ defensive	❏ intense	❏ perplexed	❏ useless
❏ delicate	❏ intimidated	❏ pessimistic	❏ valued
❏ depressed	❏ jealous	❏ powerless	❏ victimized
❏ determined	❏ joyful	❏ productive	❏ victorious
❏ difficult	❏ judged	❏ quiet	❏ violated
❏ dirty	❏ jumpy	❏ reflective	❏ wacky
❏ disappointed	❏ kind	❏ regretful	❏ warmhearted
❏ disillusioned	❏ lazy	❏ relaxed	❏ weak
❏ disorganized	❏ light-hearted	❏ relieved	❏ weary
❏ eager	❏ listened to	❏ reluctant	❏ wishful
❏ embarrassed	❏ lost	❏ resentful	❏ worse
❏ encouraged	❏ lousy	❏ resistant	❏ wounded
❏ enlightened	❏ loved	❏ respected	❏ wrong
❏ envious	❏ mad	❏ responsible	❏ yearning
❏ excited	❏ manipulated	❏ romantic	❏ young
❏ fatigued	❏ mischievous	❏ rushed	❏ zealous

5. What did you do last week to nourish your soul (that is, take care of yourself—emotions, mind and body)? What self-care will you do this week?

6. Darlene Conrad, a single mom, administrative assistant and former nurse, wrote the comical "What I Learned from My Breakdown" list below. Circle one of Darlene's statements that reminds you of an insight you've gained during your imperfect life journey. Write your own new comical affirmation in your Relief Journal.

What I Learned from My Breakdown

It hasn't always been fun. In fact, there were some very bad days. I didn't expect or plan for my life to turn out this way. Still . . . God is good. He honors my faith and never leaves me. I've learned to laugh and that's a relief! Here's what else I've learned:

- Pain is a good indicator that something is wrong. *(Pay attention!)*

- Your body will betray you and give up first. *(Self-care is vital.)*

- Accepting help is a no-brainer—which is good because your brain checks out right after your body betrays you.

- Losing something (or someone) you believe you can't live without will prove you wrong.

- Believing someone else's lies is a complete waste of time.

- As bad as it is today, it could be worse. *(And it will get better!)*

• Trying too hard to figure out *why* made my head hurt. So I stopped asking God why and asked for peace instead. *(Peace came!)*

• I can't make everything just right, but I can make it! *(With Christ's help.)*

• Disappointment from lost dreams and pain from failed expectations don't lower your standards. They improve your ability to grant grace freely. *(Whew!)*

Take a few moments to reflect on the verse below and to talk with God about what you're learning, sensing and/or feeling at the moment. Then jot down your thoughts in your journal and date it.

The LORD will guide you always; he will satisfy your needs in a sun-scorched land and will strengthen your frame. You will be like a well-watered garden, like a spring whose waters never fail (Isa. 58:11).

Dear God, You're my source and authority.
You repeatedly point out the way before me.
You fulfill my needs and expectations when I feel dried up—
and generously offer me power to live my day with
healthy thoughts and actions.
Because of You I have the promise of becoming
like a well-watered garden
full of fresh insight and fertile ideas.
Thank You for giving me strength for this day and celebration
hope for tomorrow.
(Author's paraphrase of Isaiah 58:11.)

The Relief of
Imperfect Life-Work
and Service

CHAPTER 8

When a Go-Getter Goes Haywire!

Today I'll slow down until I catch up with myself.
Enid Howarth and Jan Tras, *Daily Imperfections*[1]

"Our speaker isn't here yet," I whispered to my colleague. It was 6:55 P.M. The meeting started at 7:00.

I walked outside while my partner started the program. Scanning the parking lot, I found no sign of our speaker. At 7:07, the presenter rushed toward me in a state of controlled frenzy. "I need to make copies of my handouts and set up my Power-Point," she panted. "Where can I do that?" While she frantically worked to complete her preparations, I waited at the back of the room.

Then it dawned on me: *Joan, this is a flashback to the way you once lived. From one rush to another; one crisis to another. Jumping from fire to fire as you doused each one just in time to avoid burning your feet. You do not want to live like that again!*

Although I realize I'll never be perfectly balanced or suddenly become mistake-free, I *am* committed to facing my home, work and service-related projects with calm intentional planning and implementation. Still, I admit that occasionally I'm tempted to return to my old action-addicted patterns of work-

ing and serving and the adrenaline rush it creates.[2] This usually happens when my inner Saboteur convinces me that I'm not
doing enough or accomplishing all I'm capable of doing—I
need to try harder, work faster, make more money and rack up
more points.[3]

When an experience like the one with the harried speaker
reminds me of former exhaustingly chaotic days, I sense God's
assurance that I'm not less spiritual (or unproductive) when I
cease rushing, doing, fixing, running and overworking. That
crazy lifestyle proves nothing. I know God and I don't have to
live like that. I never want to go back to those miserable ways
again—when my go-getter self went haywire. I hold on to a
verse from Paul's letter to the Galatians:

> But now that you know God . . . how is it that you are
> turning back to those weak and miserable principles?
> Do you wish to be enslaved by them all over again? (4:9).

Not everyone is convinced that a move from chaos to calm
is the best idea, however. Recently, a colleague raced around
the corner toward me, jacket and scarf flying in the breeze,
computer bag banging against the wall. Breathlessly she announced, "I don't feel like I'm getting anything done or that
I've achieved my goals for the day unless I'm at least a half-
hour late for each meeting." She was an hour-and-a-half late
for our scheduled appointment—she must have felt real
accomplishment that day!

Anne Wilson Schaef, author of *Meditations for Women Who
Do Too Much*, poses the following questions: "What kind of
creed have we accepted that tells us that we are of no value
unless we are working ourselves to death? . . . What belief have
we accepted that suggests that, if we are not rushing and hurrying, we have no meaning?"[4]

"No" Is Not a Naughty Word

"Lord, the one you love is sick."
Yet . . . he stayed where he was two more days.
John 11:3,6

Martha and Mary sent a message to Jesus that their brother, Lazarus, was deathly ill. They wanted and expected Jesus to come to his bedside, but Jesus chose to say no (see John 11:1-6). He had a sound reason for His decision.[5]

On occasion we may decide that it is beneficial to say no to a request, even a reasonable one. With Jesus as our example, we can be assured this is acceptable. We are not obligated to say yes to make someone else feel good. Saying no may merely mean "In my opinion, granting your request wouldn't be useful at this time." We can say no without rejecting the personhood of the one making the request. The statement "No, I don't care to go out to dinner tonight" is not the same as "I don't like to be in your company." It doesn't mean that you don't care about children's spiritual education if you say, "No, I won't teach first-grade Sunday School this year." We can say no and remain loving and caring people.

For years, Karen Boothe, a home-school teacher, Christian youth theater worker and ministry volunteer, had a difficult time declining any request to serve. She didn't want to disappoint God or others by leaving a worthy task or project left undone. But she's learning the benefits in admitting she can't do it all perfectly all the time:

> The phone rang and I answered. "Karen, we have an opening for a third-grade teacher for the Wednesday night program at church," said our children's minister. "You're so good with the kids. You'd be great for this. Would you think about it and let me know?"

I had no strong desire to do this and I was already involved in several other areas at our local church. Still, I didn't want to leave her stranded—or the kids without a teacher. In years past, I most certainly would have said, "Sure, I'll do that," simply because there was a need and I didn't want to let God or His people down. But this time I said no. I had been trying to be more intentional and prayerful about my time commitments and this one just didn't seem right. I didn't have peace about it. I still felt guilty when I said no.

After my decision, I prayed that the children's minister would find a willing teacher soon. Later I learned that the woman who took the position was not currently serving in our church. The role fit her gifts and she had time to prepare, create great activities and nurture the children. My own daughter had fun in her class and learned much.

That was a turning point for me. I'm learning that God is okay with my saying no, even when saying yes would meet an important need. I don't want to hinder God's work and plan, yet that's what can happen if I accept a position based on guilt or obligation. I realize God empowers many gifted and willing people besides me. I now seek the peace of God over being the perfect—and overworked—servant of God.

Over-the-Top Prep

Rest is not a sedative for the sick, but a tonic for the strong.
It spells emancipation, illumination, transformation!
It saves us from becoming slaves, even of good works!
L. B. COWMAN, *STREAMS IN THE DESERT*[6]

Sometimes we try too hard to serve. We make over-the-top preparations and plans so that everything will be perfect. Yet just because we're asked and we *can* meet the need or fill the position, doesn't mean we *must*. God may have a different idea for our serving, working and helping. Audrey Thorkelson, an Intentional Woman presenter, speaker and Bible teacher, shares how God protected her ministry decisions, even though she didn't understand at the time:

"Audrey, would you teach your 10-week Bible study on relationships during our fall semester?" asked our ministry coordinator.

"I'd love to," I responded. Years ago, I had written the curriculum (based on Jacob's life) and facilitated it several times. I looked forward to doing it again.

"Great. Thirteen different Bible study teachers will have a booth at the Fall Kick-Off event," she explained. "Each woman who attends will choose the class she wants."

Within the next few weeks, I prayed, planned, plotted and prepared. By the morning of the 9:00 to 11:00 A.M. Kick-Off, I felt ready. I decked my display table with pretty napkins, a lace tablecloth, a plant and family photos (to represent relationships), as well as attractive folders with outlines, handouts and the proposed schedule.

By 9:00 the room was filled with women who walked among the 13 tables, each representing a different study class. My heart sank as I watched every woman walk straight past my table. Only one lady stopped just long enough to ask, "How many do you have in your class? I don't want to be in a small-sized group." *Gulp!*

This is embarrassing. Maybe I should have given door prizes. I buried my face in the large coffee mug I held so that my hands wouldn't be idle, and contemplated crawling under the table. Compounding my discomfort, a man stopped briefly and asked, "How's it going?"

"Not well," I replied.

"Well, did you pray about it?" he asked.

Immediately I felt guilt and confusion. Of course I had prayed! I felt God wanted me to teach. Just when I thought it couldn't get worse, a tall woman shouted across the room, "Funny you're teaching on relationships and no one's come. Doesn't anybody love you?"

"Obviously not," I muttered. I shuffled out the door at 11:00, feeling defeated and discouraged. The next morning I evaluated the situation.

What did I know with certainty?

- God loves me no matter what I do or don't do.
- God gave me this material and it has helped women each time I taught it.
- God has good plans for me.

What would I do next?

- Take the high road (see Hab. 3:17-19.)
- Talk to some friends and request them to pray for me.
- Ask to be released from teaching this Bible study in the fall.
- Trust God and believe He wastes nothing.

That fall when I would have taught the Bible study, we had two major family tragedies that took all my strength and attention. I had tried so hard to make my Christian service just right and couldn't understand when it didn't work out like I planned. Yet what I

thought was an imperfect catastrophe, God used to
protect and provide for me.

Just like Audrey, we may have a genuine desire to make a
positive difference in the lives of others. We long to serve, teach
and help. Consequently, we wonder if we'll prove ineffective if
we stop *doing* in order to rest or focus on personal or family
matters. We may forget that God sees from the long view—that
we can rest and trust in Him:

> Though the fig tree does not bud and there are no grapes
> on the vines, though the olive crop fails and the fields
> produce no food, though there are no sheep in the pen
> and no cattle in the stalls, yet I will rejoice in the LORD,
> I will be joyful in God my Savior. The Sovereign LORD is
> my strength; he makes my feet like the feet of a deer, he
> enables me to go on the heights (Hab. 3:17-19).

Even after many years of more relaxed thinking and behavior, I still sometimes wonder how I'll accomplish my goals if
I let up. Then I recall a legend I once read and I smile.

One morning a hunter stumbled over a man seated under a
tree and playing with a small tame bird. "Why, you're the apostle
John," exclaimed the hunter. "I'm surprised that an important
and dedicated man like you would be out wasting your time."

John looked up at the tall stranger and asked, "Why have
you left that bow dangling on your shoulder?"

"Well, don't you know?" replied the hunter. "If I kept it continually pulled tight, it would lose its spring and become ineffective."

John chuckled and said, "That's the reason I play with this bird."

The writer of Ecclesiastes captured the same wisdom this
way: "God takes pleasure in your pleasure . . . Each day is

God's gift" (9:7-8, *THE MESSAGE*). God is pleased when we loosen the tight hold we have on our lives. Enjoyment, relaxation, renewal and play are examples of His generosity. We might even accomplish more when we step back and live one day or one project at a time.

Multi-Tasking: Friend or Foe?

What a paradox that while we long for a break
from the weariness of work,
we rail against rest in our society. We want to work harder
so we can retire early and enjoy life. Yet we feel guilty
when we take time off,
worrying that people will think we're lazy,
or that someone or something
will pass us by and we'll lose our competitive edge.
MARSHA CROCKETT, *DANCING IN THE DESERT* [7]

Most of us have learned to multi-task when attempting to whittle down our to-do list, whether a mental list or written on paper. Yet we don't have to do everything all at once in order to make a significant contribution to our families, friends, neighborhoods, churches or jobs.

Even time management specialists admit that sometimes we overdo it when it comes to multi-tasking. "If you've ever attended a time management seminar, read a book about organizing your life, or picked up a business magazine, you've read that it's a big time-saver to do two (or more) things at once. I personally recommend it to my readers and the clients that I consult, but feel that there is a time and a place for everything, pros and cons to each circumstance," writes Debbie Williams in her online article "The Pros and Cons of Multi-tasking." [8]

"Try to avoid going too far in doing anything. Those who
honor God will avoid doing too much of anything."

Ecclesiastes 7:18, *NCV*

Updating your calendar or writing down your appointments while booting up your computer, or reading the newspaper while waiting on hold to make a doctor's appointment can
help you conserve time. But talking with a client on your cell
phone, handing a snack to your son in the back seat and dig-
ging for toll change all while driving down the freeway at 70 mph
is distracting, counterproductive and even hazardous. Without
a doubt, this kind of *multi* multi-tasking contributes to our
stress level and sense of overwhelm. Nancy Kennedy, author of
When Perfect Isn't Enough, describes her day when she does too
much—maybe you can relate:

> Some days I hit the floor running at 5:30 A.M. and rarely
> get everything done by 10 P.M. . . . I find myself skipping
> meals, opting instead for Krispy Kreme doughnuts and
> coffee for breakfast and whatever's 99 cents at Wendy's
> for lunch. I don't mean to, but sometimes I skip God
> too. . . . But when there isn't time for God, it's because
> time is my god and my to-do list is my master.[9]

After years of practicing the art of multi-tasking, many of
us have become quite proficient at it. Yet recent research indicates that multi-tasking lowers effectiveness, generates mistakes, jeopardizes memory, contributes to back pain, can cause
flu and indigestion, and even damages teeth and gums.[10] Multi-
tasking and overload go together like thunderstorms and light-
ning. (For the record, the dictionary defines "overload" as "to

fill to excess so that function is impaired."[11] And all this time we thought we were multiplying function!)

David Meyer, a professor of psychology at the University of Michigan, is one of many researchers working on studies that show how multi-tasking negatively affects not only the outcome of tasks but the health of the taskers, too. "The body releases hormones to cope with extra-challenging task situations," Meyer explains. "If it goes on very long—like for air traffic controllers, traders in a Wall Street pit or single mothers—it leads to brain rot."[12]

Becoming Friends with Time

To love life is to love time. Time is the stuff life is made of.

This quote from Benjamin Franklin intrigues me. Living in harmony with time. Agreeing not to compete against time. Becoming friends with time. What a relief-filled possibility!

A colleague surprised me recently when she said, "I'm in the process of changing my philosophy about time and work—and beginning to think that maybe fulfillment and success are not found in keeping my nose to the grindstone every minute. I've decided to try to be a bit easier on myself—to take breaks, to pause and talk with fellow workers and to rest when appropriate. However, I admit I feel extremely uncomfortable about this. Am I doing the right thing?"

Perhaps God allows finite human beings (that's you and me!) to live within the confines of time to protect us from anxiety overload and burnout. Changing our concept of time as a slave-driver or tyrant to that of a friend will help us become more peaceful and content. Wouldn't that be a refreshing way to live?

And I am sure that God, who began the good work within you, will continue his work until it is finally finished on that day when Christ Jesus comes back again (Phil. 1:6, *NLT*).

> *Lord,*
> *Thanks for the safety of time limitations.*
> *Keep reminding me that "no" is not a naughty word.*
> *I let go of my need to do everything and serve everyone.*
> *I'm trusting that You'll finish in me what You've started.*

CHAPTER 9

When the Going Gets Tough, the Tough Get Burned-Out

In vain you rise early and stay up late, toiling.

Psalm 127:2

"I'm calling because I need the name and address of your showroom," said the man on the other end of the telephone. "Also, would you please give me a brief description of how you work with clients?"

"Ummm," I said. "Ahhh . . . j-j-just a moment." I stared at my desk, moved around a few papers and panicked. *What's he asking? I'm not sure. Where can I find the answers? Don't know.* How I concluded the conversation, I don't remember. I'm not even sure why I answered the telephone that day. Usually that's the receptionist's job.

I sat in my office surrounded by the ever-present piles of papers and stacks of files. I was the president of a growing new company and the staff and I had just reached a potential $1 million in sales, up from $100,000 the previous year.[1] Yet to me it did not feel like success. Instead I felt like I was in a dreary prison camp. "Get me out of here!" I screamed inside. "I've gotta get out of here!" But I couldn't. I felt stuck.

The simple details in an ordinary day seemed overwhelming to me. I coped by pretending to be a machine. Before each
appointment I withdrew to my office, shut the door and went
through the motions of cranking up my brain. Once when I
forgot to close the door and an associate glanced in, I winced.

On this particular April afternoon, stuttering into the
phone, my mind simply shut down and I couldn't move the
imaginary crank. A few days after the telephone call, I realized
I could no longer gut it out. *Something has to give! Enough! I can't
keep going.* I felt fried and very un-Joan like. It was time to step
back and heed the advice of Diane Fassel, author of *Working
Ourselves to Death*: "We have to ask ourselves if our lives are
becoming unmanageable in relation to our busyness, rushing
and working."[2]

I made an uncharacteristic decision to admit my need and
see a counselor. Gradually, I began to understand that my problem was called "burnout" and it was the result of over-rushing,
trying too hard and giving in too much. I felt propelled to keep
moving, working and doing. Sixty-, 70- or 80-hour work weeks
were not uncommon. Sometimes I surprised myself when I
realized I had skipped several meals. I could not permit myself
to say no to a new job or client. Business partners, family and
customers all intuitively knew this about me and pushed my
people-pleasing button.

One Christmas season, a client called to ask me to redeco-
rate his house for the holidays. When I told him my schedule
was already full, he insisted. "You must make room for us," he
pleaded. "You've got to help me save my marriage." (Several
months later, he and his wife divorced. Like I could have kept
that from happening!)

The following bizarre conversation with a business partner
jolted me to admit my critical situation. "I'm just too tired,"
I said one day after a meeting. "I need a few days off."

"You can't right now," he replied. "We're too busy and we need you."

"What if I had a car wreck and was decapitated?" I asked. "Then you'd *have* to get along without me."

"Well, if that happened, I'd come to the accident site and wire your head back on so that you could work." He laughed, but I felt like throwing up. I had become the person wise old Solomon felt so sorry for:

> I saw something . . . that was senseless: I saw a person . . . He always worked hard. But he was never satisfied with what he had. He never asked himself, "For whom am I working so hard? Why don't I let myself enjoy life?" This also is very sad and senseless (Eccles. 4:7-8, *NCV, ICB*).

Finally in an effort to relieve the many physical symptoms of burnout and give myself time to think, I decided to take a month off. Incredibly, I ended up working 40 hours a week during that time. I really didn't think it was a big deal. I got a clue, however, when my counselor asked if he could use me as an example of what *not* to do. His comment helped open my eyes to the reality of my need. Like my friend Cathy Roberts, a women's minister, wife, mother and family/marriage counselor, I sought relief:

> I wanted to achieve something big, to make a substantial contribution to this world. If I made a big enough splash, all my hard work and sacrifice would be worth it. Then I could stop doubting myself—and others would respect and validate me, too.
>
> Each time my husband accepted a new job opportunity at a larger church, I felt a little better. We were really moving up! Then I was offered a job teaching part-time

at a university and I felt great—now I was someone important. I taught a major Bible study, facilitated parenting
seminars for local school districts, designed and taught
teacher training classes and workshops, and wrote many
parenting articles for the newspaper. *More feathers in my cap!*

But I got tired—way too tired. I felt stressed, exhausted, always behind and joyless. Somewhere along the
way, I realized I had reached my goal and made it in the
eyes of my community, state and world. Yet I had lost
my life. I hurried too much. Worked too hard. Neglected
self-care and rest. And lived under the burden of everyone else's expectations. I hardly knew my children and
had little time for my husband. Although I had everything I ever dreamed of, I felt miserable. Burnout
threatened my existence.

When I finally recognized my need and decided to
alter my self-destructive thinking and behavior, God chose
to move us to another state. I took this opportunity to
gain a fresh start on managing my schedule and learning
to live purposefully. I do not have the fame I once covet-
ed, but I *do* have my life. Whew. That's real relief.

Lest you think that burnout only happens to someone who
overworks for too long in a particular job, consider this definition: *Burnout* is the type of stress and emotional fatigue, frustration and exhaustion that occurs when a series of (or combination
of) events in a relationship, mission, way of life or job fail to produce an expected result.[3] Burnout can happen in a career, job
(volunteer or paid position), relationship, marriage, church or
ministry when you ignore healthy limits and reasonable expectations, schedules and goals.

Myron Rush, author of *Burnout: Practical Help for Lives Out of
Balance*, elaborates: "Burnout is not a respecter of persons. . . .

Doctors, teachers, bus drivers, counselors, pastors, homemakers, students—all can experience burnout syndrome. . . . Most people experiencing burnout do not have a history of emotional or mental disturbances. . . . But all people suffering from burnout are hurting emotionally and psychologically—and usually spiritually."[4]

Addicted to Action

In chapter 1, you read an overview of the three types of workaholics: (1) the obsessive worker, (2) the work binger, and (3) the work anorexic. Symptoms may include compulsive rushing and busyness, constant thinking about work or performance (even as a mother, wife or friend), continual list-making, refusal or reluctance to take time off, an inability to relax, increasingly diminished self-care and spiritual life, and procrastination and withdrawal.

"The List That Won't Die . . . In our heart of hearts, we believe the 'one thing' truly needed is a completed list! Yet no matter how hard we work to cross things off, more appear. It's like housework and paperwork. Just when we think we're done—*poof!* There's more. Why can't that happen with the good stuff instead, like birthday presents and chocolates?"

Debi Stack, *Martha to the Max: Balanced Living for Perfectionists*[5]

The narrower definition of "workaholism" is *addiction to action*. The action addict is driven to do too much, care too much and rush too much. Some refer to it as the "hurry disease." One recovering action addict said, "When I was a child, I memorized the Bible verse: 'Redeeming the time, because the days are evil' (Eph. 5:16). Eventually, I misconstrued this verse to mean I should fill each minute of every day with activity and accomplishment. Occasionally I paused long enough to realize I was not in control of myself or my time commitments. Time and circumstances controlled me. I then resolved to step back and adjust, only to be sucked up into the excessive doing once again."

There's Hope

When I dug past the burnout, I discovered a defective pattern of misconceptions. I believed the lie that I must make all things right for my family, clients, business associates and anyone else who came across my whirlwind path. I believed that I must appear perfect so that others would be attracted to my God. I believed that it was my responsibility to see that my husband was always happy, healthy and satisfied with life. "Peace at any cost" and "Don't rock the boat" were my unspoken mottos. All my time and energy was involved in fixing life so that it would work for other people, and simmering under the surface, I was angry at not being permitted to be the person I thought God wanted me to be. The *me* God created got lost in the action-obsessed maze. To erase the pain, I used my own detrimental ways of managing my life (*mis*-managing is more like it).

Many days I wanted to run away and hide. I longed to know if it would be all right with God if I decided to change my habits, slow down and relax. I wondered if I could still be a productive and valuable person if I stopped trying to do and make everything just right. Then one night (after a strangely revealing dream) a light flicked on in my brain. I realized it wasn't escape from my life or relationships that I wanted, but a changed pattern of thinking and behaving *within* my life and relationships. This was a turning point for me.[6] With a sigh of surrendered relief, I prayed, "God, I've been trying to do and be what I can't without You. I admit this hasn't worked well for me. *Please* help me." With God as my partner, I slowly began to accept my limitations and imperfections. Brigita Bilsens, a regional vice president, went through a similar process:

> It is a daily challenge for me to balance my work, family and friend time, but I'm improving and so grateful. During the last two years I've been promoted twice and am now being told I might lead the company one day. Previously I felt monopolized by my career and it negatively affected my physical, mental and spiritual health. (I ended up with cancer, although I've now recovered.)
>
> This time with my expanded responsibilities, I realize I *cannot* be perfect. Not everyone will like me all the time; at times I'll disappoint. I won't get it right every time and sometimes I'll have to work with those I don't agree with. I have so much I could stress about that I need to actively put it in perspective so that I won't derail again. I'm even more comfortable with my personal imperfections as I work on making intentional changes like weight loss. I can't do it all, but I can do what I can do. I'm making imperfect progress. God and I are working on this together.

In *Breathe: Creating Space for God in a Hectic Life,* author Keri Wyatt Kent writes about Dr. Brent W. Bost, an obstetrician-gynecologist in Beaumont, Texas, who contends that "there are 60 million women in America who are so overscheduled and overstressed that it affects their physical health."[7] This backs up my belief that we face an action-addiction epidemic within our communities, work places, churches, schools and families. I see it weekly in my coaching, speaking and Intentional Woman contacts. Today I spoke with five coaching clients who admit to dealing daily with their own version of trying-too-hard-to-make-it-just-right. Each one is committed to finding relief in the midst of her imperfection, just as Lisa Gifford, a wife, mother and former burnout victim has:

> For most of my adult life, I juggled multiple jobs. Real estate agent. Corporate employee. Bookkeeper for three companies. Multiple investments manager. And all the while, I was struggling to save a difficult marriage, be a good mother, maintain numerous unhealthy relationships, keep a spotless house, remodel the investment properties, think fast and stay on top of my to-do list. (Sometimes I wrote down a task just so that I could check it off!)
>
> No more! I just read through my personal journals of the last few years and felt sadness, peace, joy and accomplishment! Yes, accomplishment—for doing less!

Journal entry, three years ago:

> Lord, at times I desire more financial opportunities and work success. Other times I simply want to be home for my children, husband and myself. I'm tired. I love fun, but I'm not having any. I don't want to be here anymore.

Journal entry, several months later:

> Lord, I've cried until there are no more tears, still I can't get rid of the pain. I'm not who I want to be, but I don't know who that is. I've lost Lisa. It's been four years since I was faced

with the heart-wrenching truth (and lies) of my marriage. I thought it would be better by now.

Journal entry, later that year:

> I can't do it anymore. I'm disappointed and angry at how my life has turned out, especially since I've worked so hard. I want to go to sleep, but can't. Everything is rush and hurry. I want to be alone, but can't. Bruce leaves when the kids don't cooperate and there's too much to do. I've had it.

Journal entry, one year later:

> Today while at the doctor office for my seven-month pregnancy checkup [with my third child], I made a list of everything I'm doing currently—work, house, investments, kids, marriage. The doctor asked, "How are you doing?" And as tears filled my eyes, I handed him the list.

Journal entry, today:

> By God's grace, my life changed that day in the doctor's office. I quit my corporate job and the investment properties, and hired a bookkeeper. I rarely, selectively (and with help) sell real estate and I've set boundaries on relationships and home projects. I'm not the angry, stressed out, disappointed person I used to be. I don't secretly blame my husband anymore. When I ceased my financial over-doing, Bruce rose to the challenge of providing for our family. It's a

process and not always perfect, yet I smile when I realize God lovingly granted my desire to multi-task by giving us our fourth child last year! We named her Grace. God is good. I do feel accomplishment—for doing less!

No Longer Lost

One of the main characteristics of workaholism
is that it is a process run wild.
It's about rushing, pushing, intensity and so on.
If we attempt the same process with recovery,
it will elude us every time.
There simply isn't a quick fix for work addiction.
We may as well learn now that we are always going to be recovering,
because recovery is learning to live in process.
DIANE FASSEL, *WORKING OURSELVES TO DEATH*[8]

I became so wrapped up in the daily routine of cranking out work that I lost me. I didn't know myself anymore. The person I thought I knew was buried under layers of smoldering ashes. The "together" image I saw in the mirror encased an emotionally dying woman.

It sounds over-dramatic, but it's true. The question that haunted me was, *Can I be found?* I didn't know when or if I'd ever come back. Yet, step by step, little by little, God picked up the burned-out fragments, repaired them and pieced them back together.

God knew where I was all the time. He never stopped thinking about me. And when the time was right, He reintroduced me to myself. Then when I could handle it, He showed me how to change my self-destructive lifestyle so that I wouldn't get lost again. I'm amazed and relieved by God's love. And God loves, sees and hears you, too. Tell Him what you need.

How precious it is, LORD, to realize that you are think-ing about me constantly! Search me, O God, and know my heart; test my thoughts. Point out anything you find in me that makes you sad, and lead me along the path of everlasting life (Ps. 139:17,23-24, *TLB*).

You restored me to health and let me live. Surely it was for my benefit that I suffered such anguish. . . . For the grave cannot praise you, death cannot sing your praise . . . The living, the living—they praise you, as I am doing today (Isa. 38:16-19).

Lord,
How great is Your love!
You know me inside and out.
Please share Your thoughts with me.
And help me be the calm person You designed me to be.
I know You alone can restore me to healthy living,
working and relating.
I'm partnering with You.

Relief Reminder

Before reading the next section, "The Relief of Imperfect Churches and Culture," take a break and play through the Relief Guide for Imperfect Life-Work and Service. You may do it alone or invite someone to join you.

The Relief of Imperfect Life-Work and Service

After reading chapters 8 and 9, please respond to the following questions and exercises in your Relief Journal.

1. Which story, anecdote or illustration in chapters 8 and 9 hit closest to home? How so?

2. I felt relieved when I realized it wasn't escape from my life or relationships that I wanted, but a changed pattern of thinking and behaving *within* my life and relationships. What's your personal response to this idea?

3. Reread the definition of "burnout" in chapter 9. Rewrite it in your journal *in your own words*. What part of the burnout definition strikes a chord within you?

4. Burnout can happen when we adopt unrealistic expectations and strive for *perfection* instead of *excellence*. For those of us who try too hard to make it just right, it's often helpful to see the difference between perfectionism and excellence. Read through the Excellence vs. Perfectionism Chart on the next page and circle the words or phrases that describe you at times. Relief can move in when we become aware of the thinking and behavior that works against us. You may wish to do this exercise with one of your specific roles in mind, such as worker, friend, mother, wife.

Life Categories	Excellence . . . • is enjoying quality in balance (possible). • operates *for* me.	Perfectionism . . . • is the relentless chase for perfection (impossible). • operates *against* me.
Life is shaped on . . .	the pursuit of being.	the pursuit of doing.
My self-talk sounds like . . .	I want, I wish, I would like, I will, I can.	I must, I should, I ought to, I need to, I have to, I never.
My motivation is . . .	to emphasize the positive; a desire for achievement.	to avoid any negative; a fear of failure.
I expect . . .	the best of myself.	to be the best in comparison to everyone else.
I'm controlled by . . .	self-responsibility before God.	other people's opinions and reactions, past and present.
I feel . . .	*free*—in pursuit of excellence.	*confined*—in a prison of perfectionism.
My predominate emotion is . . .	contentment, satisfaction.	fear, a sense of failure.
My satisfaction occurs . . .	throughout the activity.	only at victory.
My focus is on . . .	the process.	the finished product.
The price I pay is . . .	hard work.	overwork, stress, burnout.
Winning is . . .	good, but not required.	mandatory for survival.
Losing is . . .	disappointing, but manageable.	devastating.
Short-term, my work . . .	satisfies others.	satisfies others.
Long-term, my work . . .	pleases others.	causes alienation from and discord with others.
The benefit of my work is . . .	sustainable, long-term success.	short-term success.
The outcome of my work is . . .	accomplishment, acceptance, fulfillment, success.	disappointment, condemnation, frustration, failure.
I perceive life as a . . .	challenge that is welcomed.	curse that is dreaded (endured).
I dwell in . . .	reality, the real world.	a fantasy, an unreal world.
The possibilities are . . .	many colorful options. I have choices.	limited to all or nothing, good or bad, black or white.
The bottom line is . . .	THE TRUTH: People, organizations and things do not have the ability to be flawless. Life doesn't have to be perfect to be wonderful.	A MISCONCEPTION: People and things have the ability to be perfect. Life and others are a continual disappointment.

5. What did you discover while reviewing your Excellence vs. Perfectionism Chart? Consider sharing your discoveries with a friend or partner.

Take a few moments to reflect on the verse below and to talk with God about what you're learning, sensing and/or feeling at the moment. Then jot down your prayer in your journal and date it.

Satisfy us in the morning with your unfailing love, that we may sing for joy and be glad all our days. May the favor of the LORD our God rest upon us; establish the work of our hands for us—yes, establish the work of our hands (Ps. 90:14,17).

Lord God, only You are perfect.
I'm not.
My family's not.
My job's not.
Even my service isn't flawless.
Still I know You delight in my work and love me unfailingly.
This makes my heart sing.

The Relief of Imperfect Churches and Culture

CHAPTER 10

When Bigger-Better-More Squeezes Out Life

In a world of chaos, problems, heartache, and anxiety, all of us need peace.

Linda Dillow, *Calm My Anxious Heart*[1]

I roll over and glance at the blinking numbers on my bedside clock: 5:15 A.M. *Joan, you'd better get with it. You need a head start if you're gonna finish all you must do today.* I drag myself out of bed, slip into my sweat suit and head into my home office. After journaling, praying, checking my email and adjusting my computer-generated to-do list, I make a protein drink and skim the newspaper.

When the early morning clinic opens, I call for results of a recent medical test. Yesterday after three recorded messages, I never did talk with a real person. Behind schedule because I spent two days "healing" a virus that shut down my computer, I feel internal urgency listening to two phone messages I must address before my 1:00 P.M. meeting. I'm babysitting my precious grandchildren tonight (bright spot of my day!), have appointments this morning, meetings all afternoon and a project deadline looming.

JC, you don't have time for your walk this morning. Get real! I wince when I hear the familiar inner voice reminding me, *You'll never catch up, Joan.* (Ugh! I hate—okay, intensely dislike—the recurring battle with my inner slave-driver.) This morning I silence her by yanking on my walking shoes and setting off toward the community center near our house.

As my walk takes me past the all-purpose room, I see leftovers from last night's party. (I didn't go, of course. No time for that.) Like a magnet, the old piano in the corner pulls me inside the empty ballroom. Then I hear that same inner voice: *Joan, What are you doing? You're going to play this out-of-tune spinet with half the keys missing when you have a shiny black baby grand just steps from your office? You haven't played that piano lately—what's the massive draw to this one?* I scrunch my forehead at the question I can't answer, pivot and power-walk out the door.

Surprised by an intense sense of sadness, I head home. I feel like crying, which is unusual—tears don't come easily for me. *What can I do? I have deadlines, responsibilities, commitments, money to earn. No time for pleasure or creativity right now.* I despise the troublesome possibility that burnout threatens again.

After stretching on the patio, I open the back door to see rapid-fire combat scenes on TV. I stare at the beautiful olive-colored faces of young sisters (my granddaughters' ages) weeping over their father's body. The reporter standing in the Jeep shouts above the roar of war. I think of my friends and colleagues in the Middle East and Central Asia. Since leaving my last job, I no longer travel to work with them, yet I miss them intensely. Massaging the knot in my neck, I pray for them and our soldiers.

Back at my computer, three forwarded emails predict I'll have a lousy day—and that I don't truly love the sender—if I neglect to forward them to 15 more people. (Not going to happen! I reassure myself this does *not* mean I don't love the person sending the email.) I discover several legitimate requests among the SPAM. A fax arrives as a UPS delivery lands on my front porch. I ignore the IM message that dings in.

With 20 minutes before my first client call, I grab my journal and scrawl these words: *overwork, overdo, overachieve, overstimulate, over-control, over-know, over-think, over-feel, over-help, over-care, overextend, over-shop, overspend, over-eat, over-exercise, over-diet, over-expect, over-impress.*

I write faster and in large, capital letters: *MEDIA OVERLOAD, INFORMATION OVERLOAD, TECHNOLOGY OVERLOAD, SENSORY OVERLOAD, SPORTS OVERLOAD, DEBT OVERLOAD, PEOPLE OVERLOAD, WORK OVERLOAD, CELEBRITY OVERLOAD, SEXUAL/BODY IMAGE OVERLOAD, NOISE OVERLOAD, CHURCH OVERLOAD, SPIRITUALITY OVERLOAD.*

Tossing my pen, I mumble, "It's over-everything!"

You and I are swimming in an ocean of over-choice and over-exposure. Jane Chesnutt, editor-in-chief at *Woman's Day* magazine calls it the "over-scheduled, over-worried, over-whatevered life."[2] And there's no sign that it will ever let up. Steve Farrar, author of *Overcoming Overload*, writes, "There is no more room in our lives. Yet every new day brings more commitments demanding to be squeezed in."[3]

After sharing my piano-walk-overload story during a recent workshop, a woman shouted, "Yes!" Soon everyone at her table stood to cheer. They didn't applaud their maxed-out reality, but the fact that someone had verbalized what they felt.

Our culture pushes the limits as far as possible and then pushes again. Even our churches seem to adopt a viewpoint that perfection (and limitlessness) is mandatory and attainable. It's like we honestly believe we can do bigger-better-more-faster and keep it up forever.

Beyond God-Designed Boundaries

We live in a day of shallow superlatives.
Entertainers and athletes perform feats hailed
"the greatest" by the world.
But truly great human endeavors are those done for Jesus . . .
And they bear the mark of eternal excellence.

DENNIS J. DEHAAN, *OUR DAILY BREAD*[4]

"From activity overload to choice overload to debt overload to expectation overload, we are a piled on, marginless society," writes Richard A. Swenson, MD, in *The Overload Syndrome*. "Overload is that point when our limits are exceeded."[5]

We thrust more and better everything into our 24-hour days: more and better work, more and better activities, more and better information, more and better equipment and computers, bigger toys and houses, more money, more leisure, more hobbies, more health and better bodies, more and better relationships, more faith and bigger, better churches and more and better service. And as Tina Henningson, a wife, mother and Intentional Woman presenter, shares, bigger-better-more-faster churches can sap both energy and the joy of service:

> I belong to a mega church—with its exploding membership, countless programs and outreach opportunities, massive influence, and world-famous pastor. It's been wonderful. Yet sometimes I'm overwhelmed by the bigger-than-life approach.
>
> I hear, "Everyone needs to go on a mission trip outside the country." But I'm not led to go at this season of my life and I feel guilty. Friends testify, "This trip changed my life" and it compounds my guilt. When pastors introduce another new small-group curriculum

and strongly suggest we attend, I feel uncomfortable not signing up. We've helped with many building programs over 23 years, but not this time and I feel wrong saying no.

Approaching the empty-nest season, I prayed, "God, show me if this is the church where you want us now."

God seemed to say, "Tina, you can't do everything and I don't want you to. Listen to your heart and My Spirit's inner nudging. Don't worry about the church's agenda for you or anyone else. Trust My agenda for you. We'll do it together."

Now I serve with relaxed joy and not from a sense of guilt—in the church office, with the spiritual gifts program and in a women's Bible study (where we choose our own curriculum). God answered my prayer: *Tina, stay and serve on My terms, just where you are—in this church. Live free.*

The truth is, we have the same limitations of time, space, energy and desire as do all humans. This will not change. Yet some of us live as though we don't believe limits exist. Sometimes we let culture, churches and schools persuade us to live and work beyond our God-designed human boundaries. We may even bully ourselves into expecting to work and accomplish flawlessly. And when we don't, as journalist Allison Sebolt found out, we may have a hard time keeping reality in perspective:

Set to graduate *magna cum laude* from a major Midwestern university's school of journalism and be inducted into the journalism honor society, I tried to relax and enjoy the celebration. But I couldn't, because I faced a huge dilemma. As an editor for a city magazine the journalism school produced, I went online to check that week's issue. Immediately I noticed a mistake: I had accidentally switched the attribution of two quotes in a sidebar containing inspirational quotes.

I panicked. *How could I do this? I'll get a lower grade. All for some silly error. I can't let that happen. I've worked too hard for four years!* Endeavoring to hide my emotions from my roommate, I hid in my closet.

But I didn't feel right not admitting to something that was my fault, so I emailed my "confession" to my professor, the teacher's assistants and two other editors. Then I continued to obsess about the potential impact it would have on my GPA, blowing it completely out of proportion. I felt unworthy to graduate with such honors, and it robbed part of my joy as I walked across the stage and ate dinner with my family.

Back in my room, I checked my email and felt my heart pound when I saw my professor's message with my final grade and evaluation. I scrolled to the bottom and stared in disbelief at my grade: the first letter of the alphabet without so much as a minus attached to it. The attached note read: "The incident from yesterday did not affect your grade. Enjoy your work."

When I could finally think clearly again, I realized how my perfectionism (*I should never make a mistake!*) blurred my hold on reality and almost squeezed the life out of my graduation celebration. Even if the error *had* lowered my grade a bit, it wouldn't have been enough to disqualify me for the honors I received.

Through this uncomfortable situation, God taught me that (1) its okay to admit my mistake(s), even when they are minor and might go unnoticed, and (2) God gives me room to make mistakes and grow from them. In the midst of it all, He loves me.

Something Backfired

For every hour progress saves by organizing and
technologizing our time,
it consumes two more hours through the consequences,
direct or indirect, of this activity.
Because this fact is counterintuitive and subtle,
we do not recognize it happening.
DR. RICHARD SWENSON, *MARGIN*[6]

Living in a culture that wants it all and wants it all perfect, we can start to expect what isn't possible and feel entitled to more. We didn't think this would happen. Researchers and inventors guaranteed that progress would ease our harried personal lives and work schedules, making our days happier, easier and less chaotic. In some ways, it has. Computers with features like spell check, cut and paste, clipboard and merge mean I rarely use White-Out anymore. Continually improving email processes, instant messaging and global cell phones mean I can communicate with friends, colleagues and staff immediately, even though our time zones are 3 to 13 hours apart.

"The world is now producing nearly two exabytes of new and unique information per year. Don't feel bad if you don't know what an exabyte is. No one does. It's a new term, one they had to coin for a billion gigabytes."

Kevin A. Miller, *Surviving Information Overload*[7]

Paradoxically, we expect more. We have less time to get answers and procedures completed and returned, and must postpone other creative projects to meet our looming deadlines.

We generate longer to-do lists. New technology that came as a result of progress was supposed to mean less paper to review, file or trash, but it doesn't. Life is busier and more complicated. Something backfired.

A business owner in a neighboring city recently reported, "To stay in business, I had to chop our working budget almost in half and lay off several employees, including the assistant manager. This means the remaining staff must double-up on duties and projects with no time and compensation to match. Because we must produce more goods in less time with reduced manpower, we have little energy, resources or hours to brainstorm, reflect and create the new products we need. We used to work long hours during a special project, but now it's constant. Tension's thick around here." Sadly, this appears to be the increasing norm rather than the exception.

Longing for Answers

Jesus resumed talking . . . tenderly. "The Father has given me
all these things to do and say. This is a unique Father-Son operation,
coming out of Father and Son intimacies and knowledge. . . .
But I'm not keeping it to myself; I'm ready to go over it line by line
with anyone willing to listen."
MATTHEW 11:27, *THE MESSAGE*

How can we learn to live gracefully and gratefully in the midst of this imperfect and overloaded reality? When I attempted to read and pray about it, my brain turned mushy; the search became part of the overload. Something more added to my to-do list.

Then one afternoon I sat alone on a white wicker swing, surrounded by colorful flowers (I love that!) and read Matthew 11:28-30: "Are you tired? Worn out? Burned out on religion? Come to me. Get away with me and you'll recover your life.

I'll show you how to take a real rest. Walk with me and work with me—watch how I do it. Learn the unforced rhythms of grace. I won't lay anything heavy or ill-fitting on you. Keep company with me and you'll learn to live freely and lightly" (*THE MESSAGE*).

I read the words silently. I read them aloud. I reviewed the text leading up to Jesus' words. Suddenly something clicked inside me. *Joan, this invitation is from Me to you. I am God. I told Jesus what to say. Everything He said and did while on Earth came out of our unique relationship. Listen to His words as though I'm speaking directly to You.*

"I'm listening, Lord," I wrote in my Bible's margin. I read Jesus' message again. Could this be the realistic solution to the bigger-better-more-faster dilemma? Might I discover relief from this relentless-pursuit-of-perfection culture? According to Lorraine Aldermann-Testa, a school administrator and sorority volunteer, it *is* possible:

> I just wanted to be loved, popular and respected. I figured the way to reach my goal was to be the perfect daughter, wife, sister, teacher, administrator and servant/helper—all while having the picture perfect look.
>
> I had a plan for accomplishing this goal. Here's how it worked: I saw other women who I respected and defined as successful. Each seemed to do a multitude of important things simultaneously. I determined that to be successful—therefore admired and loved—I must be as busy as I assumed they were. If I thrilled at the thought of doing something, it was God's will and I pursued it. If I saw a need and I could do it, it was a sign I should. (However, if I felt I couldn't be perfect with a project, I didn't try.)
>
> After each accomplished goal, I thought, "Now I'll be happy, loved, and valued." Instead, I felt shallow, empty

and afraid. *Lorraine, you're not there yet. You'll never be remembered. Do more. Work harder.*

After several God-enlightening experiences, I started a search for the Lorraine God designed—not the perfect woman I tried to create. Then about 18 months ago, I realized a life-long dream to be on the board of directors for my college sorority. Again I faced that familiar doubt: *I'll never do this right.* So nervous that I felt physically ill, I couldn't fully celebrate. I sensed God wanted me on this board, yet felt overwhelmed.

Instead of retreating or trying too hard to please, I decided to face the challenge intentionally this time. My life coach and I determined visual aids might help, so I used simple sticky notes—on one I wrote DOABLE and on the other, REASONABLE. When afraid I might make a mistake or appear inept, or when I wanted to voice my opinion or volunteer for a project, I'd glance at the sticky notes and ask, "Is this doable? Is it reasonable?" When uncertain if I had the time, energy or resources to accept an assignment, I asked the same questions. If I answered yes to both questions, I moved ahead with confidence. Gradually that old self-defeating "avoid mistakes at all costs" fear began to lessen.

My doable-and-reasonable tool worked so well for me in the board of directors job that I now use it to help me with decisions at work and at home. I have new beliefs: *God does not demand that I accomplish the impossible. God has no unrealistic expectations for me. God's teaching style doesn't include trying to "trip me up." I can relax.* My doable-and-reasonable tool helps me gauge whether a decision I'm making is based on the perfect Lorraine or the real Lorraine.

I've stopped trying so hard to be someone I'm not. God loves me for *me.* My doable-and-reasonable job is to have faith that God has good plans for me. I'm realizing God loves me just the way I am, imperfections and all, and that it is through the sacrifice Jesus made on the cross that I am able to have a personal relationship with God.

Reviewing Matthew 11:28-30, I noticed something I'd never seen before: Jesus' unique offer to come, get away, walk, work, watch, learn and keep company with Him covers every area of my life—self-care, life-work, finances, education, relationships, marriage/romance and spiritual growth. Although I can't stop the escalating cultural overload, I can come to Jesus for relief in the midst of it, sometimes even getting away with Him for silence and solitude.

"For I know the plans I have for you," declares the LORD, "plans to prosper you and not to harm you, plans to give you hope and a future" (Jer. 29:11).

Lord,
I accept Your offer to partner, learn and relax with You.
Thanks for not pressuring me with unrealistic expectations.
Guide my daily decisions with family, life-work,
self-care, church and friends.
I want to listen to You instead of the
bigger-better-more-faster culture around me.
I'm going to pause to find rest in You.
Please show me how.
I'm watching.

CHAPTER 11

That's Not How It's Supposed to Be

*Then Jesus said . . . "I have come that
they may have life,
and that they may have it more abundantly."*
John 10:7,10, NKJV

"Joan, we're glad you decided to follow Jesus," said Mom and Dad one afternoon when I returned home from school.

"Me, too," I responded with a smile. I flashed back to several weeks before when Dad leaned over after a church meeting and asked if I wanted to ask Jesus Christ into my life. Indeed, I did. (Even at that young age, I *longed* to know God.)[1] That night, I told God I believed Christ died for me and that I wanted to give Him my heart, mind and future.

"Daddy and I know you want to serve God," said Mom. "We think it'd be good for you to learn to play the piano. It's a way to honor and serve Him as you get older."

Within days I met local piano teacher Mrs. Teeter at her studio and started my love affair with music. Practicing almost every day, I made progress for the next 12 years. I played for choirs, bands and musicals at school, church and Youth for Christ.

But my hands were too small to play octaves and I couldn't play by ear like my friend Patty. When I accompanied, I had to read the written notes, and sometimes needed to practice in order to do my best. (Imagine!) I felt flawed even though I loved playing and was told I had a special touch for interpreting the music. I wanted to play without cheating to look at the song book (that's how I saw it). Over time, I developed an embarrassing nervous twitch when I played. Sometimes my knees shook so hard they jarred the entire piano.

Nothing here on this earth is perfectly perfect! Not our service, talents, desires or thinking. Not our churches, pastors, programs, ministry strategies or worship. In fact, I'm not even sure what perfect looks like. One church member thinks perfect music is when everyone follows the written notes in balanced harmony. Another believes perfect is when the music leader ad-libs the lyrics and tune while singing. We can't even agree on perfection!

Imperfection, Misunderstandings, Abuse and Disillusionment

> *God redeems all our blunders, all our stupidity.*
> *The crucial choice is choosing God over not choosing God.*
> LESLIE WILLIAMS, *NIGHT WRESTLING* [2]

I'm grateful for my strong Christian heritage. I enjoyed—actually cherished—the opportunity to serve, worship and grow up in church and parachurch settings. (I know you may not identify with my childhood experiences. That's fine. You have your own unique story. God values us both!)

During those years, intermingled with the good, I received some misguided messages. Here are two: (1) Everyone should always be on the same page and never express opposing (defined as negative) opinions, thoughts or emotions; and (2) each

Christian worker and pastor must be super-human, consistently meet impossibly high standards, teach or preach with superior knowledge, and persistently perform with warmth, wisdom, humility and tolerance all the time and in every way.

That's a little exaggerated. Still, the expectations were quite high.

I recall numerous tragic illustrations of the truth. Spiritual leaders not only have human needs, limitations and imperfections (just like people in the congregation), but some also have deep unexamined emotional wounds that compel them to treat others—and themselves—poorly. Ecclesiastes 9:2 says that "both good and bad things happen to everyone" (NCV). We may wish it were not so, but it is.

Our past disappointments and pain influence how we make decisions and interact with others. Combine this with the fact that we all have different temperaments, passions, gifts and ideas, and it's no wonder leaders in Christian organizations and churches experience interpersonal challenges that often result in misunderstanding and distress.

Pastor and author Peter Scazzero believes there's a connection between emotional growth and spiritual maturity and that our churches (pastoral staff as well as individuals in the pews) need to address this in order to love freely, live joyfully and grow to be healthy followers of Christ. He writes, "The link between emotional health and spiritual maturity is a large, unexplored area of discipleship. We desperately need, I believe, to reexamine the whole of Scripture—and the life of Jesus in particular—in order to grasp the dynamics of this link."[3]

Sadly, sometimes Christians (visible leaders or those behind the scenes) hurt—and even sin against—the people they're trying to serve. Names have been withheld from the following story to protect everyone involved, but perhaps you can identify with some of the painful details:

My husband and I loved worshiping and serving in our church. He was an active lay leader and I worked on the staff as director of a growing ministry within our local congregation. For over a year, we prayed with the pastoral search committee as they looked for a new pastor. Everyone felt grateful when the new minister and his family finally arrived to give us positive direction for the future.

It didn't take long for me to notice that everything wasn't working exactly as hoped. Things happened that just didn't add up for me. Our staff and the pastor seemed to have a difficult time negotiating strategies for church development. I asked for explanations about the new methods and programs he used to initiate spiritual growth. I wanted to understand his reasoning and ideas, but when I asked questions and voiced concerns for the men and women in my ministry sphere, I felt discounted and misunderstood. The effective methods we previously put into place were pushed aside. It confused many and a heavy cloud of gloom seemed to fall over the pastoral staff.

It seemed the more I looked to Scripture, the more confused (and agitated) I became—our church's new reality didn't seem to match up with what I knew to be true of God's Word. I began to feel spiritually and emotionally abused—and I'd never been in a situation like this. I confided to my supervisor and felt his support. Yet he said his hands were tied.

After praying and talking together, my husband and I decided to leave the ministry we loved. Just as our first child was born, we said goodbye to a lifetime of relationships—spiritual grandmas, grandpas, aunts and uncles we'd planned to share with our little one. Our hearts broke as we abandoned our dream for our family's spiritual future. We set off as nomads looking for a new church with our new bundle of joy and our unwanted bundle of pain. This was not what I had planned for myself or my family. It was not the way it was supposed to be. Our pain ran deep. Still does. We lost much.

"Doesn't someone owe you something? An apology? . . . An explanation? . . . A childhood? . . . A marriage? . . . People in your past have dipped their hands in your purse and taken what was yours," writes Max Lucado in *The Great House of God*. "Jesus does not question the reality of your wounds. He does not doubt that you have been sinned against. The issue is not the existence of pain, the issue is the treatment of pain."[4]

I have a deeply committed Christian friend who left her church several years ago after some spiritually/emotionally abusive incidents and has not returned to that church or any other. Another friend whose faith remains strong is burned out on church and its leaders. "I've seen behind it all and it isn't pretty," he says when asked about his withdrawal. I feel sad for both friends, yet I recognize their hurt and respect their choices.

My friends aren't alone in their disillusionment of the church and its leadership. George Barna, the respected pollster and author of *Revolution*, predicts the percentage of Americans who receive their "primary means of spiritual experience and expression" from the local church will drop from 70 percent in 2000 to 30 to 35 percent by 2025.[5] Imperfect churches. Imperfect leaders. Imperfect people in the pews. What can we do? There is no quick or easy answer.

Beginning to Forgive

Jesus said, "Father, forgive them,
for they do not know what they are doing."
LUKE 23:34

What if the person we need to forgive is one we are supposed to respect? What if the one who harmed us is a parent, teacher, leader, spouse or minister? Forgiving may seem like an impossible task. Smoldering anger and resentment at someone who hurt me contributed to my workaholism and burnout. I wanted to forgive, but it was difficult. In the book *Forgive and Forget: Healing the Hurts We Don't Deserve*, Lewis B. Smedes' insight helped me: "The highest respect you can show people is to let them take responsibility for their own actions. Love has . . . the power to let people be responsible for hurting us. Love does not forever find excuses for them, or protect them."[6]

We may find it hard to admit that people who we're supposed to trust have abused their power. We may have been taught that "honoring those in authority" means to do what you're told, never question, criticize or disagree, keep the peace no matter what, and hold your tongue if things start to look or feel really bad. But God is pleased when we admit the truth, even about our hurts. Facing reality releases us to begin forgiving. Joseph didn't excuse his brothers' wrongs after they threw him in a pit and left him for dead. But he intentionally chose to forgive (see Gen. 50:15-21). We can be honest about how others have hurt us as we pray the way Jesus taught us: "Forgive us our debts, as we forgive our debtors" (Matt. 6:12, *NKJV*). And we can be honest about our own mistakes, as Cheryl shares:

> I wanted to feel loved, accepted and secure. But I never
> did—not as a child, teen, grown-up, Bible teacher, foreign

missionary or pastor's wife. I tried to be good so that my parents would love me, but it didn't work. After I met Jesus Christ personally, I worked hard to follow the biblical rules, thinking this would give me the perfect life. Yet I always felt like I failed, if not in action, then with what I judged as faulty thoughts and emotions like anger or fear.

Tired of it all, I crumbled. Painful memories of past abuse surfaced. No one understood. Then I talked with a Christian therapist who helped me realize that in my pursuit to please God, I missed His grace. She reminded me that I can't obtain the perfection God demands, yet He sent Jesus to sacrifice for my need—only because God's Spirit lives in me am I worthy of His love. I had taught this amazing truth, but hadn't yet internalized it.

As I began to let God love me, deeply buried pain emerged. A voiceless scream exploded within me. Each time the scream sounded, I ran. To cope, I figured out a way to silence the scream: *Cheryl, you must connect with someone.* Because I never felt love from my mom or dad, I longed to be held in the arms of a mother-figure where I'd feel safe enough to cry. I replayed every good memory like the times when a kind woman would listen, care or hug me. I now realize I used connection with motherly women in a similar way that alcoholics use alcohol or workaholics use work: to silence the pain.

At about that time, I met a woman who cared about me with that strong maternal-type love. My faith grew through her mentoring, but I became emotionally dependent on her; being with her took away my pain. She became an idol and things went awry as our emotional and spiritual connection led to physical and sexual intimacy. Eventually our relationship caused incredible pain and we ended our friendship.

I turned to another woman for comfort. Sadly, this relationship took a similar turn, even though we both remained committed to God and His service. Just as before, the results brought deep hurt and turmoil. When the awful realization of what I was doing hit me, I was flooded with shame. It is a paradox I still cannot understand—I remained devoted to God the entire time.

I lost my reputation, ministry, friends and church family. Most refused to listen to my pain and doubted my confession and repentance. Some chose not to forgive me. My utter sense of brokenness felt unbearable. One friend from my church remained loyal, walking many long, excruciating miles with me.

In this dark, awful place, God's love beamed. I stopped running away to my false fix and finally faced my fear and anger. My life is not a she-lived-happily-ever-after story. I still struggle against shame and deep regret for my mistakes and sin. I lost position, respect and many friends. But I found my heart's longing: love, joy and peace. No longer striving to please God, I now stand before Him with a broken heart and open hands, praying: *Lord, if You can and if You want to, You can use me.*

Acceptance and Release

It takes a profound conversion to accept that God is
relentlessly tender and compassionate toward us just as we are—
and not in spite of our sins and faults, but in them and through them.
BRENNAN MANNING AND JIM HANCOCK, *POSERS, FAKERS, AND WANNABES* [7]

For one who loves words, I find it difficult to respond in writing to Cheryl's story, to respectfully acknowledge her pain—that which she caused and that which was unfairly thrust on her. Hurt people hurt people, even when they don't want to. We live, work, worship, play, share, give and love in the midst of imperfection, injustice, misunderstanding and unadorned human-ness.

Cheryl's last sentence touches a raw nerve in my soul: *Lord, if You can and if You want to, You can use me.* It is as though Cheryl is praying, "If You can and want to use me—even in light of my past—I'm willing, Lord." It's a prayer born of surrender, vulnerability, release and acceptance that nothing will ever be perfect and that God is worth trusting—not out of fear, but out of love wrapped in relief. It is a realization that "no sin is great enough to drain dry the ocean of God's grace."[8]

In this chapter, we read the experiences of three unique women. The first, a seminary student ministering on a church staff, shares how deeply she was hurt by a spiritual leader's actions. The second woman, a pastor's wife and Bible teacher, tells a story filled with longing, sin and restoration. The following story of a professional woman, Cathy Roberts (who is now a director of Women's Ministries and serving alongside her husband as he works on an international missions team) shows how fear of hurting others—by not serving perfectly—can strangle joyful service.

By the time I was in my mid-30s, I sensed an annoying companion peering over my shoulder. I called her the Phantom of Perfection. She made my life as a pastor's wife quite stressful, constantly shaming me into believing that I had done something to offend or hurt somebody in our church.

Every time I tried to ignore the Phantom, she whispered more troubling messages in my ear. *Cathy, what if your pastor husband does something to offend someone? That would be terrible!*

I spent incredible amounts of physical and emotional energy trying to hush the Phantom by making sure everyone stayed happy. If someone wasn't pleased, Phantom of Perfection assured me it was my fault. Finally I couldn't take it anymore: I crumpled under the pressure and became very angry at everyone else for making me feel so awful.

The Phantom was filled with unrealistic expectations that contributed to my burnout-induced misery. I spoke with a wise mentor who helped me recognize some of the sources of my everything-must-be-just-right thinking. Eventually I realized that only *I* could silence this tyrannical Phantom of Perfection. By choosing not to do so, I was actually creating and perpetuating my own burnout.

Although my pastor husband and I both desire to lead with love, we cannot guarantee the spiritual growth or happiness of the people we serve. To try to do this impossible task only keeps others from leaning on God for their power and joy. I accept my human limitations and imperfections and ignore the Phantom that kept me in bondage. What a relief to let God be God and stop trying so hard to minister just right.

Some things we will never understand, like why God chooses to partner with imperfect, limited human beings; who God calls to lead; why some spiritual leaders abuse and hurt others; how people can study and memorize Scripture and then disrespect God's children. It doesn't make sense to us. *It's not how it's supposed to be.* Yet we heighten our pain when we silently insist that other Christians (especially our leaders) must be perfect, doing things just the way we believe they should. And we increase our stress when we insist that just because we long to, we should serve others flawlessly.

"God never meant for us to be afraid. . . . It breaks God's heart that we are afraid of him, afraid of life, afraid of each other, afraid of ourselves."

Brennan Manning and Jim Hancock, *Posers, Fakers, and Wannabes*[9]

We may try tirelessly to build an earthly utopia for our churches, families, fellow Christians or ourselves, *but it is not possible*. The truth remains that life is often harsh, unfair and confusing—full of trembling-knees-and-shaking-pianos experiences. We're human, and sometimes we fail to live up to our own unrealistic standards. Sometimes our spiritual leaders hurt us. What can we do? How can we get up and go on?

It's not easy. We hurt beyond imagination. I think of the story and testimony of Lisa Beamer, wife of Todd Beamer who was killed by terrorists September 11, 2001, on Flight 93. Interviewed several months after that tragic day, Lisa said that this was not what she wanted for herself or her children—and God knew that. What prevented her from hysteria was knowing the truth: In the end, eternity was still okay, even if the here and now wasn't. She concluded by saying that the foundations of her life were still intact.[10]

God's promise of a perfect tomorrow can help restore our will to live today, as well as our ability to forgive the painful yesterdays. It's an imperfect process. Some days we feel like forgiving. Other days we don't. Although we cannot see it and we cannot touch it, we can hope. And hope is what we need to provide a reason to awake each morning and breathe through one more day with God.

Do not let your hearts be troubled. Trust in God; trust also in me. In my Father's house are many rooms . . . I am going there to prepare a place for you (John 14:1-2).

Relief Reminder

Before reading the next section, "The Relief of Imperfect Dreams, Plans and Decisions," take a break and play through the Relief Guide for Imperfect Churches and Culture. You may do it alone or invite someone to join you.

The Relief of Imperfect Churches and Culture

After reading chapters 10 and 11, please respond to the following questions and exercises in your Relief Journal.

1. Briefly review the over-the-top expectations of our culture. How has this over-everything mindset affected you? Your family? Your life? Your church?

2. Which story or illustration in chapters 10 and 11 touched you most? In what way?

3. It's a relief to admit we can't do everything, go everywhere or help everyone. Saying yes to one thing means we will say no to something else. And when we say no to a task, request or invitation, we then have the opportunity to say yes to something else. (It might even be yes to resting or spending time with a friend!) Use the following chart to help you choose when to say yes or no concerning a current decision. (Example 1: In order to say yes to helping my daughter with her house work and three little girls [after she broke her foot], I said no to making dinner and finishing up a project at home. Example 2: When my friend agreed to attend a breakfast meeting, she said no to her morning walk.)

By Saying Yes to . . .	I'm Saying No to . . .
1. _____	1. _____
2. _____	2. _____

By Saying No to . . .	I'm saying Yes to . . .
1. _____	1. _____
2. _____	2. _____

4. How do you feel about the story and testimony of Lisa Beamer at the end of chapter 11? What is your ultimate hope?

Optional Exercise

Jot down the name of a person you'd like to forgive. It may be someone in your past or present, or it could be yourself. Write a letter to that person, telling him or her how you feel. Then put the letter aside. Re-read the letter in a few days. Add to it if you'd like. Then let it sit a few more days. Read it again. Don't send the letter. At some point, destroy the letter. (*Suggestion*: Feed it into a shredder and watch it get gobbled up!) Take a few moments to reflect on the verse below and to talk with God about what you're discovering, sensing and/or feeling at the moment. Then jot down your prayer in your journal and date it.

> Oh! May the God of green hope fill you up with joy, fill you up with peace, so that your believing lives, filled with the life-giving energy of the Holy Spirit, will brim over with hope! (Rom. 15:13, *THE MESSAGE*).

Dear Lord, my ultimate hope is in You.
Please give me wisdom to determine when to say yes and when to say no.
Grant me courage to reach out and forgive, as You forgive me.

The Relief of
Imperfect Dreams, Plans
and Decisions

CHAPTER 12

Hey, the Sky's Not the Limit!

When today is less than perfect, I will remember that I survived yesterday.

Enid Howarth and Jan Tras, *Daily Imperfections*[1]

"Joan, would you come out to the garage, please?" asked my husband, Richard, last Saturday morning. "I need your help."

On my way down the hall, Richard said, "The garage door broke."

"You're kidding me, right?" I said. But when I got out there, I saw it was no joke. The garage door hung crooked—about four feet off the ground on one side and almost touching the floor on the other side. What a morning for this to happen! It was the day of our annual Webb Invitational Golf Tournament.

"Here, hold this cord while I try to pull the other cable," Richard said. We soon determined fixing it ourselves was a lost cause. "We'll have to call a repairman," he concluded.

Not only did we have a golf tournament starting in one hour, but we also had 60 people coming for dinner on our patio at 4:30 P.M. Richard needed to be at the course within the next five minutes to register the golfers. I was supposed to meet my daughter-in-law so that we could take photos of all the guys as they teed off for 27 holes of golf.

Richard hurried to the kitchen pantry and reached to the top shelf where we kept a three-ring binder with telephone numbers of all the companies who worked on our house when it was built. As he retrieved the appropriate book, another one fell and hit a large glass bottle of soda, which crashed to the tile floor sending chards of heavy green glass flying through the air across the counter and into the hall and living room. Liquid oozed over the kitchen floor.

I knew Richard and our house guest (both playing in the tournament) needed to leave in order to make it on time. "You go. I'll find the number and call the repairman," I said. They left in the golf cart as I sloshed through the sticky puddles.

I found the garage door company's business card and left a message for someone to call on my cell phone. I tackled the clean-up job and then hopped in the car that Richard had parked in the driveway the night before. Very unusual, but a good thing he did—at least it meant I had wheels. The other car was stranded behind the broken garage door.

When we all got to the golf course, we discovered that the manager had planned for the wrong starting tee time, which threw off the schedule and lunch time. That meant I would have to deliver box lunches to the golfers while they played instead of having them do lunch at the Grill.

The garage door repairman called and I met him at the house. After shuttling back and forth between the repairman and the clubhouse several times, he called to tell me he had completed the job: The garage door now hung straight.

I wrote him a check for his services and then, hurrying to return to deliver the lunches, I pressed the garage door button so that I could run under it as it closed. I knew I must jump over the sensor so that the door would continue its descent, but in my haste I jumped too high at just the wrong time. *WHACK*. It didn't immediately dawn on me what had happened until I dropped to the ground in pain. *POP*. (There went my neck!)

"Do not boast about tomorrow, for you do not know what a day may bring forth."

Proverbs 27:1

Suddenly the repairman appeared at my side. He had been in his truck headed down the street. "I heard the noise," he said. "Are you all right? Can I call someone for you?"

"Whoa, that hurts," I admitted. "Is it bleeding?" I lifted my hand to the top of my head and felt no blood. "I'll be okay. I've got to get back to the course," I said as I wobbled to the car.

By this time, I concluded I was being filmed for the *Candid Camera* show, but no one jumped from the bushes! The irony was that we had worked on the plans and preparation for this special day for an entire year. We prepared meticulously.[2] We covered all our bases. Yet all that careful planning didn't halt these irritating surprises. Sometimes circumstances and situations just get messy beyond our control.

But maybe that's okay, as Teresa Perrine, the Women's Director for Campus Crusade for Christ at Arizona State University and an Intentional Woman presenter, suggests:

> For several years I've focused on being intentional about serving God as the person He designed me to be instead of concentrating on what others (or my inner slave-driver) think I should do. Working the Intentional Woman five-step process helps.[3] Yet lately it seems every time I try to make purposeful decisions, my legs get knocked out from under me. I'm taking time-outs and thinking before I say yes, but it still isn't enough. When I mentioned this to my life coach, she asked. "What's happening?"

"Well, I'm living intentionally and life is *still* messy," I replied. "Whoa, I think that's what confuses me."

"Tell me more," she said.

I paused to let it sink in. "I gotta admit it's disappointing. I think I believed that if I lived intentionally, I would always be relaxed."

"Just what does 'intentionality' look like for you?" asked my coach.

"Intentionality is paying attention to the three questions in Step One: (1) What's good about my life? (2) What concerns me about my life? (3) What is missing from my life?[4] I constantly check in with these questions to assess whether I'm living wisely and using my giftedness. Each night I review my concerns and voids. But now as I think about it, I realize I emphasize concerns and voids and minimize the good."

"What do you mean?"

"I'll always have things that concern me or are missing in my life. If I focus only on these, I'll never relax," I said as I stopped to gather my thoughts. "You know what? Just dawned on me: My concerns are often management-type issues that can be dealt with tomorrow or assigned to someone else to take care of."

"Your voice and breathing are slowing down," observed my coach. "What's up?"

"Yes, I noticed it, too," I replied. "Interesting. I chose the word 'acceptance' as my 2007 spiritual growth focus. I think I'm beginning to see that along with all the good, I'll always have some messiness, concerns or voids. This actually brings me some relief. I don't have to keep relentlessly trying to figure it all out and make all things perfect. I want to learn to relax in the midst of messiness," I continued. "With university students coming and going at the house, my campus work, the needs of four children, my husband and my home, it's overwhelming at times. For example, every year at this same time we have workshops and mentoring on Sex and the College Student. I hear so many painfully messy stories. It's heavy. I get exhausted. But I wish I didn't."

"Teresa, if you weren't drained by it all, you'd be God."

"Hey, thanks. You're right. I'm *not* God. Whew!" I chuckled. "Imagine acceptance and surrender producing relief. I can still be intentional without trying so hard. Reminds me of Matthew 6:34. It's like God is saying 'I'll take care of your tomorrow, so you can enjoy the good in today.' Helps me relax a little more."

Unrealistic Expectations and Dreams

So position yourself completely in My care, and let go of all those things you cannot control. Then you will find true peace.
SHERI ROSE SHEPHERD, *HIS PRINCESS: LOVE LETTERS FROM YOUR KING* [5]

"Dream, work hard and everything will be yours. The sky is the limit! You can do anything you want to do," concluded the commencement speaker as the students and parents rose for a standing ovation. But can we do *anything*? Will *all* dreams come true?

Newlyweds plan a large family but discover they can't conceive. A young man's dream of being a pilot dashes when he loses his eyesight. We can plan, pray and work, but some dreams will not come true. Their fulfillment is beyond our control. [6]

Other things may be within our personal control, but not within the realm of human possibility: After working 10 hours at the office, a mother plans to cook dinner, attend a son's concert, sew a costume for her daughter's play and still get a good night's sleep. How realistic is that? Not very! Perhaps we need to rethink what we've been told. Hey, is the sky really the limit?

The oft-quoted Philippians 4:13 claims, "I can do all things through Christ who strengthens me" (*NKJV*). Sometimes I think we use Bible verses like this one to back up an unrealistic belief that God will help us do everything we long to do whenever we want to do it in the perfect way we envision. But God does not require or expect us to do *all* things. He knows our human limitations. After studying the original meaning of these words in Paul's letter to the Philippians, I've concluded that this seems a reasonable rendering of his statement: *All that God wants (or asks) me to do, I can do through Jesus' power*. It's a relief to know I can grow into the person God designed me to be, rely on His strength, and trust that He is the one who makes right what sometimes seems so wrong.

Recently I contacted a friend I hadn't seen for a while and asked if she would consider sharing what she's learning about accepting her singleness. Brigita, a regional vice president, responded immediately with the following relief-producing email message:

> Joan, believe it or not, I'm finally at the place where I embrace God's plan for me—which at the current time includes being single. I trust that I'm in the center of His will doing what He created me to do, like Esther "for such a time as this"(4:24).
>
> Perhaps at a different season of my life, He'll bring me my husband (or maybe not). But today God has called and enabled me to seize the moment and enjoy the blessings of singleness. I'm doing that with remarkable peace!
>
> I've also relaxed the unrealistic expectation that I must be the perfect weight or achieve a specific level of

financial, professional or community status in order to be loved by a man. I now believe that my husband (if he is to be) will love me just how I am. I feel free to be comfortable in my own skin. I'm relieved I can be myself.

As I get older (43 now), I place more value on my health—body, mind, soul and spirit. I want to stay connected to God and allow Him to help me make wise choices about how I spend my time and energy. I've worked so hard all my life and although I've gained much, slaving away is exhausting. Now I'm committed to getting good results while working fewer hours and expending less emotional energy. I'm convinced this is what God wants from me and that it will protect and enhance both my professional and personal life. I don't want to be stuck, exhausted and burned-out. This is an ongoing process for me and I'm trusting God in this journey we've started together.

Imperfect Choices and Experiences

First pay attention to [wisdom], and then relax.
Now you can take it easy—you're in good hands.
PROVERBS 1:33, *THE MESSAGE*

When I read Brigita's email, something released inside me. Her words reminded me of an imperfect (although not directly wrong) past choice I made. Over the years it has bothered me—I've perceived it as negative, yet now I'm not so sure. I know this is part of my life story, but because it bugs me, I often try to hide it.

Brigita's words of acceptance helped me see that perhaps I'm where I am today (writing, teaching, coaching) *because* of this past decision. I even wonder if maybe God ordained it for the greater good. I don't quite know how to explain it yet. But I do feel relief seeping into my soul as a result of this new awareness.

I'm reminded of biblical characters who made imperfect yet God-ordained choices to partner with God. By God's design, Hosea chose a prostitute for his wife (see Hos. 1:3), Stephen died a martyr's death (see Acts 7:54-60), Jesus' mother was willing to be rejected by friends and family (see Luke 1:34), John the Baptizer agreed to live sparsely in the desert (see Matt. 1:19), and Jesus' delay prompted Mary and Martha to experience the pain of their brother's death (see John 11:1-12:19). Although none of these situations were perfect or pleasant, true good resulted.

We do have a choice about how to respond to disappointing and imperfect experiences. It's not always easy or comfortable. Sometimes it takes months or years to work through, yet God asks us to start trusting one day at a time. We may doubt one moment and believe the next. The process is inherently imperfect, as Jen Smith, a hair stylist and ministry volunteer, learned:

> We wanted a baby, our own child to care for and love, so my husband, Scott, and I made the decision to try infertility treatment. We rode an emotional roller coaster, high on hope one day and plunged into disappointment the next.
>
> Scott and I discussed our boundaries—what we were willing to do and what we would not do. We're glad we did—we soon learned that the driving purpose of the clinic's medical staff was to get me pregnant at any cost. *What about a sperm donor? Will you donate your leftover eggs?* It would have been so easy to get caught up in our perfect dream of having a perfect baby and neglect asking God what He wanted for us.
>
> We did go through the *in vitro* treatment. Scott gave me the shots. I just couldn't do it. I cried after each one,

not because it hurt but because of what it represented. *Lord, why do we have to go through this?*

The night my eggs lay in a petri dish in downtown Chicago, I prayed, "Father, please protect our family." Looking back it seems strange that I didn't ask for twin girls or even one healthy infant. I just wanted God to protect us. He did. We had no babies.

God sheltered us that night—perhaps from having a stillborn or severely disabled child. Twins? Triplets? Quads? I don't know. He would have sustained us whatever happened. Yet I trusted God and He did exactly as I asked: He protected us. God's answer was no. We didn't get our perfect baby dream fulfilled, yet God did what was best for us.

One Thing Is Sure

Surely God is my salvation; I will trust and not be afraid.
The LORD . . . is my strength and my song.
ISAIAH 12:2

If we expect that because we work hard enough, we will know guaranteed success; and if we suppose that because we give much, we will be rich; or if we assume that because we eat healthy and take care of our bodies, we will never be sick, then we are certainly headed for a disappointing surprise. We live in a world where the future is not always predictable—or controllable.

Our carefully calculated plans may not come to fruition as we hoped. We may not see our dreams become reality. Sometimes we don't know the best decision to make. Only one thing is certain: God is our salvation, strength and song in the good, the bad and the disappointing. He is worthy of our trust.

In the morning, O LORD, you hear my voice; in the morning I lay my requests before you and wait in expectation (Ps. 5:3).

Lord God,
All nature reports to You.
You can do anything.
On the other hand, I can't reach the sky.
It's a relief to admit.
I once grabbed for "it all," now I want only what
You plan to give me.
I'm waiting expectantly.

CHAPTER 13

No Fair Comparing Sufferings!

We can make our plans, but the LORD determines our steps.

Proverbs 16:9, *NLT*

"You say God knows what He's doing and it's always good? Yeah, right! I don't see how!" is what Nick Vujicic, a young Australian man born without arms or legs, says his parents thought on the day he was born 24 years ago.

After delivering Nick, the nurses cried and hid him from his mother, a nurse who did everything just right while pregnant with her first child. When Nick's father, who is a pastor, saw his son, he ran from the delivery room, leaned over and threw up. For four months after taking baby Nick home from the hospital, his parents wept, questioned and grieved. The people in their church mourned with them. "How could this be?" they asked God.

"There's no medical reason for Nick's disabilities," explained doctors. Nothing made sense. Yet during those first few months, God gradually supplied Nick's mother and father with courage, strength and wisdom. They attempted to pass that hope to Nick, but while in grade school he became depressed. Many assumed that because he suffered severe physical disabilities, he was mentally disabled as well. Not so. The taunting from classmates overwhelmed him. He pleaded with God to give him arms and legs, crying himself to sleep at night. He despaired for his future, and wanted to die.

I saw Nick Vujicic share his story on national television.[1] "It's not my ability, but my availability," he said. At the age of 15, Nick read a Bible story about a young man born blind (see John 9:1-6). Jesus' followers asked why, and Jesus responded, "It is not this man's sin or his parents' sin that made him be blind. This man was born blind so that God's power could be shown in him" (John 9:3, *NCV*). After reading Jesus' response, Nick's heart came alive. Jesus said the blindness couldn't be blamed on anyone or anything—the tragic situation would show God's power and bring worthwhile results.

"I felt God saying, 'Nick, everything's going to be okay.' That's the assurance I longed for." From that moment, Nick decided to let God be God—of his past, present and future.

Worthwhile results? That's an understatement. Nick completed college with a double degree in accounting and financial planning. He learned self-sufficiency, typing more than 43 words per minute with the small foot he calls "my chicken drumstick." In recent days, Nick Vujicic has toured 12 nations sharing the story of God's love and transforming power to crowds numbering more than 100,000 people at a time. Nick and his team watch as tens of thousands commit their lives to Jesus Christ. Watching Nick on TV, I was impressed with the expression on his face. I've never seen a more sincerely engaging smile on anyone—with or without legs and arms. It's obvious that he truly believes Romans 8:18: "For I consider that the sufferings of this present time are not worthy to be compared with the glory which shall be revealed in us" (*NKJV*).

"If I can trust God with my circumstances, then you can trust God with yours," shared Nick. "We can't and should not compare sufferings. We all know how it feels to be lonely or broken." No matter who you are, what you've experienced or how your dreams or plans are crushed, Nick insisted, God knows you and cares. "Every detail in our lives of love for God is worked into something good" (Rom. 8:28, *THE MESSAGE*).

Perhaps you have a dream, plan or vision that has not come true and you don't understand why. Just like Nick's parents, you prayed, hoped and prepared. You've done all the right things, yet your dream remains unfulfilled. How could this be good? It just doesn't seem fair! You're disappointed, hurt, angry or maybe even in denial like Kelli Gotthardt, a Christian yoga instructor and Intentional Woman presenter, was when her dream didn't come to fruition as she envisioned it would.

I had a dream—a perfect dream based on God's perfect will for me and my family. The dream? Once I had children, I would never have to work outside the home again. In this way, I would be the ideal mother and pastor's wife.

My husband, Richard, asked if I'd be willing to work part-time if we decided to start our family. I agreed, knowing God would surely provide a way for me to stay home. When I did get pregnant, Richard and I both rejoiced.

I worked for a large corporation with thousands of employees in six locations around the country. While pregnant, I pioneered an agreement to become the first person in management to keep the position while only working part-time. Although I believed I'd never work again after the baby came, I acted as if I would.

While on maternity leave, I remained in such denial about returning to work that I neglected to look for childcare options. *How could God refuse my godly desire?* I could not envision the possibility. The night before I was scheduled to return to my job, I finally realized it was really happening. I had no babysitter, so I called a friend who took care of my baby while I reluctantly searched for permanent childcare and settled into my working reality.

I had the perfect dream, yet God had a different vision. Once back at my corporate job, I had the privilege of assisting numerous other working mothers in moving to part-time and job-share management positions in the company. I led seeker-type Bible studies for co-workers, including my boss. Several colleagues came to know Jesus Christ as Savior as a result of these Bible studies and my interactions with them. (One is Lisa Gifford, whose story is in chapter 9.)

I admit God's idea proved superior to my perfect plan. During my days on that job, I developed the skills and contacts that propelled me into my current role as speaker-trainer-consultant. Now as our children (two sons and a daughter) get older, I enjoy the freedom and flexibility to plan my schedule around their increasing needs. Also, God certainly knew me better than I knew myself back then. Knowing how miserable I get when I have too much unstructured time, He lovingly provided my job to help keep me sane and balanced. God is bigger than my short-sighted plans, and He used those early work experiences to prepare me for our current ministry together.

A Better Idea

Our shattered dreams are never random.
They are always a piece in a larger puzzle, a chapter in a larger story.
Pain is a tragedy. But it's never only a tragedy.
For the Christian, it's always a necessary mile on the long journey to joy.
LARRY CRABB, *SHATTERED DREAMS* [2]

I climbed the steps to my upstairs room and flopped on my bed. After weeks of inner prodding, I prayed, "Okay, God, I'll go where You want me to go, do what You want me to do, and be what You want me to be." Lying on my stomach, listening to the silence, I continued, "If You're calling me to Your service, I'll not hold back. Here I am."

For me, this was not a junior higher's passing fancy. From that day, I purposed to be in full-time Christian ministry. Our school district required every ninth grader to write a "future career" paper upon completing personality- and interests-assessment tests. After interviewing missionaries and Christian workers, I completed a term paper titled "Living My Dream in Christian Service."

I studied and memorized Scripture, served in several church groups and parachurch organizations, prayed for direction, enrolled in Bible School and fell in love with God. This was not something I *had to do,* but something I *longed to be.* I dreamed of being a pastor's wife and joining my husband in God's service. On December 31 many years ago, I married Richard, the love of my life. (He planned to be a pastor, but at the time of our wedding he was in his last year of a three-year stint with the U.S. Army.)

"Hope deferred makes the heart sick."

Proverbs 13:12

For almost 12 years, I lived my dream as a pastor's wife. Then one day Richard invited me to lunch and shared his plan to leave his ministry position. Stunned, I sat in silence. I could have asked more questions, but I didn't. My dream shattered into a thousand sharp pieces within my heart. I hated the pain, so I denied my disapointment, told myself God must have changed His mind and ran head-long into overworking in business. Seven years later, I ended up on the ash heap of burnout. Resentment, regret and disappointment joined me in the smoldering pile. *I didn't plan this. What went wrong?*

Looking back now, I realize it wasn't my fault or my husband's fault—and certainly not God's. I had envisioned the way God's call should be played out, yet God had a different plan. One day while studying the story of Abraham and Isaac (see Gen. 22:1-19), I saw what God wanted me to do. "Joan, give Me your dream, plan and vision," God's Spirit nudged. "I'll show My power when you relax your control."[3] I sacrificed my imperfect dream so that I could discover God's purpose for me. Adjusting our perspective—to trustingly observe our lives from God's view—can change everything, as Cheryl King, an elementary school teacher, found out:

> "Cheryl, you're flaky and irresponsible. You can't even complete college." I had never said these unkind words aloud, only to myself. I heard the inner message often enough that I truly believed them.
>
> Things changed the day I worked on my Life Plan with facilitator Joan Webb.[4] After jotting down key events from my life on a flip chart, we began listing any positive qualities or gifts we noticed in the process. I listed several, then to my surprise Joan added the word "persistence."
>
> "Why?" I asked.
>
> "Because you never gave up on finishing college," replied Joan.
>
> Tears well in my eyes even now as I remember. I never thought of it that way. After all, it took *17 years* to complete my degree. Yet Joan is right: I didn't give up. Over the years, I adopted such unrealistic expectations for myself—perfection—that I could not evaluate my

reality correctly. It's like I ignored the fact that I was in the middle of a huge snowstorm, but still considered it a moral failing for not making it to the store. How ridiculous! I can't compare myself and my circumstances to others and their situation. They finished sooner, but I couldn't and had valid reasons.

It's a happy new perspective for me. What I saw as negative is actually positive. What I previously used to berate myself with is now precisely what God uses to love and encourage me.

Fill My Cup, Lord

LORD, you have assigned me my portion and my cup;
you have made my lot secure. The boundary lines have fallen for me
in pleasant places; surely I have a delightful inheritance.
PSALM 16:5-6

Years ago when I asked God to fill my cup, it seemed instead He ate my lunch. As I saw my dreams fade, I worked harder to hold on and eventually burned out. I wondered where God was and why He let it happen. Now as I reflect back, perhaps God could not fill my cup because I already had it full with my personal agenda. I wanted to accomplish great things for God, but I had my own ideas. Maybe He waited for me to empty the unusable contents so that He could pour in His satisfying plan.

When we release the tight hold we have on our dreams, plans and visions and ask God for help, it's like emptying our life cups. Emptiness, though uncomfortable, is a necessary prerequisite to filling. Our overflowing cups often yield anxiety and confusion, while God's portion produces relief-filled security, joy and power. And though not guaranteed earthly perfection, we are assured a "delightful inheritance."

Relief Reminder

Before reading the next section, "The Relief of Imperfect Faith, Prayer and Spirituality," take a break and play through the Relief Guide for Imperfect Dreams, Plans and Decisions. Do it alone or invite someone to join you.

The Relief of Imperfect Dreams, Plans and Decisions

After reading chapters 12 and 13, please respond to the following questions and exercises in your Relief Journal. Remember that you always have the option to respond *Yes, No, Renegotiate* or *Later*. (See "Read This First!" for more explanation about these options.)

1. Explain how a story or illustration in chapters 12 and 13 made an impression on you.

2. Read Sarah La Scala's, a single mother of two, story below. What stands out to you? What can you take away from her experience?

   A neighbor asked me to join a neighborhood Bible study. I hesitated—more than hesitated. "Are you sure you want me?" I asked. "I'm not very involved in my church and don't attend the same kind you do." It was scary for me to even think about going.

   "Yes, we want you to join us," she assured me. "It doesn't matter what church you go to. Please come." So I did.

   She let me share what was on my heart and mind with confidentiality. She and others in the group brought dinners over and helped with the children. She never told me what to do.

That group of loving ladies was important for two reasons. One, I desperately needed to talk. Two, I desperately needed to listen.

While growing up, I attended church and believed in God. Didn't everybody? But I began to see the differences between just going and living spiritually. (I'm still learning, by the way). I'd never stopped to consider the real Bible message. It amazes me that God willingly sent His only Son and sacrificed Him for me. Me! Wow, that's powerful.

During this time, it was extremely difficult for my family and me. My husband, Gino, had been diagnosed with cancer. We did everything we could: traveled far for treatment, tried alternative methods, spent our savings and held out hope he'd be cured. But in the end, I lost my husband.

God showed me I had a choice: I could whine away my days or enjoy every day—the good and the not so good. I chose the latter. Now the memories of my time with Gino are rich and full of life. I believe every decision lead me to this moment. Not that I don't cringe at some past choices I made. And certainly the children and I miss Gino. But everything—my marriage to Gino, our life together, our children and his illness—are all wrapped up in the decisions I made. To regret one means the others wouldn't have been.

I don't know the answers to why, and I don't need to know. I can let that go and live my life. How liberating is that?!

3. What have you dreamed or planned that hasn't worked out as you envisioned? What does that disappointment or lost dream look like to you? Make a drawing that shows how

you feel about it or what it reminds you of. (Stick figures are okay. Flawless artwork is not required for this project! Use colored markers, pens or pencils if you like. No rules!) Share the artwork with another friend or partner who will share her artwork with you. Explain what your drawing means to you, then ask your friend what she sees in your drawing. Ask her to share her artwork and then tell her what you see in her drawing. Listen to one another without offering answers, Scripture or judgment.

4. Read Philippians 4:6-7 in your own Bible. Then read the paraphrase below. Spend some time thinking about this passage, and then write your own paraphrase, in your own words.

> Don't fret or worry. Instead of worrying, pray. Let petitions and praises shape your worries into prayers, letting God know your concerns. Before you know it, a sense of God's wholeness, everything coming together for good, will come and settle you down. It's wonderful what happens when Christ displaces worry at the center of your life (*THE MESSAGE*).

Take a few minutes to pray and share your dreams, thoughts and feelings (whether pleasant or unpleasant) with God. Jot your honest prayer in your Relief Journal. Listen for God's response(s) and consider writing down what you think He's showing you right now.

> *Lord, please show me how You've worked*
> *and are working*
> *in my dreams, plans and decisions.*
> *I want to live in the power-filled relief of my story.*

The Relief of
Imperfect Faith, Prayer
and Spirituality

CHAPTER 14

Numb and Number— When Trying Too Hard Dulls Your Soul

Don't be so hard on yourself, My love.
I see your heart filled with frustration. . . .
The battles in your mind belong to Me,
so don't waste any more time tearing
yourself down.
I love you no matter what.
Love,
Your King and your Grace

Sheri Rose Shepherd,
His Princess: Love Letters from Your King[1]

"It's the strangest thing," said my husband. "I stepped up to the tee box, shrugged my shoulders, said 'So what?' and hit the ball. Surprise! I actually played better golf. Imagine that."

"Hey, that's great. Glad you had a good game. What happened?" I asked.

"Well, lately I've noticed that when I position to hit the ball, I mentally try to control the course, maneuver the bunkers, craft a better swing, even visualize different pin placements," he shared. "That wasn't working. So today I just glanced at my golfing partner and said, 'It doesn't matter.' My relaxed attitude worked! I had a good game."

"Terrific," I said. "That's a great illustration of what my book's all about: relief from trying too hard to make it all just right!"

"Yeah," he replied. "How about that?"

Trying too hard can dull your golf game. Perhaps you've experienced this yourself or watched someone else struggle with this common problem. "Consider what happens when you're on the practice range with a driver, trying to hit the ball as far as you can—let's say 250 yards," writes business consultant Alan Fine. "Although you try very hard to hit the ball a long way, your best effort barely crosses the 200 yard marker. With only six balls left, you give up and decide to relax and just enjoy hitting them. You're not trying to hit them a long way—you're simply having fun. What usually happens? Your muscles relax, you coordinate your swing and your ball sails past the 250 yard marker."[2] Fine uses the game of golf to illustrate how trying too hard to meet unrealistic expectations can actually frustrate efforts and sabotage success in business. This same principle works in other creative endeavors, as well.

"I'm learning that 'swinging easy' can be a central metaphor for living in and from the 'sweet spot' of life."

Jon Leland, speaker, blogger, golfer[3]

Years ago I learned to knit and noticed something: When I tried too hard to make each stitch even (and, well . . . perfect), the scarf or socks or sweater shriveled, looking lopsided and squished. When I squeezed the needles and over-handled the yarn, the result wasn't pretty!

Trying too hard to knit just right dulls the finished product. Trying too hard to hit a perfect shot dulls your golf game. And trying too hard in your spiritual life—to accomplish flawless quiet times and Bible studies, gain impressive amounts of knowledge and become the perfect Christian—can dull your soul. Becky Brown, a wife, mother of preschoolers, and ministry volunteer, learned this the hard way:

> During a recent workshop for our Moms Group, we discussed the somewhat foreign notion of self-care for women of God. Our topic for the morning? "A Woman and Her God: Enjoying God More, Struggling Less."
>
> As we discussed the possibility that we try too hard with our quiet times and church involvement, one young mother said, "What? How can you have too much Bible study?" Her honest question resonated deep within me. I couldn't remain silent. So I told her my story:
>
> For years I spent so much time trying to be the perfect wife, mother, daughter, friend, servant and child of God. I really longed to please God and, well, just be *better*. I felt God wanted more from me. I attended a ladies Bible study, a women's group reading a book on marriage, another moms' group at church, and a married kinship group. In addition I intermittently facilitated a neighborhood workshop for women and helped organize and lead several of the groups I mentioned. This while mothering my two preschool sons, maintaining my home and beginning a small home-based business. It was all worthwhile, because I so wanted to learn and grow.
>
> But I became extremely tired, overly emotional and increasingly depressed. The harder I tried to grow, following all the instructions in the books about being a servant and better person, the more I ran myself down—

straight into the burnout pit. With so many studies assuring me that I should please God and make everyone else happy, I neglected my own care. Where was Becky? Ignored and gasping for air. It really bothered me that I lacked peace and I didn't feel close to God anymore.

The burnout symptoms and the depressive thoughts scared me. I couldn't help anyone, especially myself. I felt out of control and desperate. I needed help, so I met with a mentor who listened to me share my unrealistic expectations and frightening emotions. We called it "over-living." Often I try too hard to be just right with my spirituality, faith and family. I realize that if I don't take care of me, I might never become the person God designed me to be. Living on empty leaves me with nothing to give out and certainly no way to fill up my own tank. So I took several intentional steps: visited my doctor, stepped away from some responsibilities, and began spending time just for me—without family.

It's a continuing journey. I admit I struggle. I know God loves me and plans good things for me, yet I'm conditioned to over-do and over-live. Yes, I know a person can attend too many Bible studies and try too hard to pray and serve. I don't like feeling numb. I just want to relax with God and listen to His voice calming me down.

Relaxing My Grip

Peace penetrates the relationship when we are content
to waste time with God and rest in His presence.
JAN JOHNSON, *ENJOYING THE PRESENCE OF GOD* [4]

When we focus primarily on knowing *about* God, we add to our to-do list. Yet as we concentrate on *enjoying* God—being with

Him, in His presence—we begin to relax and appreciate Him. (We also learn more *about* Him. Isn't that ironic?)

When I really listen to my inner longings, I admit that I'm concerned (well, anxious) that I'll never have enough. Enough of what? *Everything.* Enough knowledge, acceptance, security, significance, goodness, hope, gentleness, love, joy, peace.

The psalmist wrote a song and the lyrics include these restorative words: "Be still and know that I am God" (Ps. 46:10). This hope-filled promise encourages me to quit holding so tightly, relax and settle into deeper intimacy with Him—just like Mary Jane Farr, a small-business owner and ministry volunteer, is learning to do:

> My spiritual walk has focused on trying to be a good Christian woman, doing what I should and avoiding what I should not. I love learning truth, so this led me to Bible study groups year after year. I studied intensely for hours and attended two to three studies a week. I believed I must amass more information in order to be able to speak the truth and "have an answer in and out of season" (2 Tim. 4:2, *NASB*). My personality is such that I love to dig deeper and study, but it became exhausting.
>
> Then I attended a weekend retreat focusing on *hearing God.* It felt foreign and I wondered if it was too mystical. Yet God began to transform my heart. I cried out in sheer frustration, "Lord, I long to be close to You." I felt His response: "Mary Jane, I just want you to spend time with Me, not study *about* Me."
>
> I now know it's not about the must-dos. And I feel transforming freedom in just *being* with Christ—heart to heart.

Imperfect Faith

*Always remember that nothing you do or say
will ever change My love for you.*
SHERI ROSE SHEPHERD, *HIS PRINCESS: LOVE LETTERS FROM YOUR KING* [5]

Doing to the neglect of *being* produces numbness. We can try and try, but it remains highly unlikely we'll ever achieve perfect faith here on Earth. John the Baptizer's depressing circumstances seemed insurmountable. Would he ever be released from prison? Did anyone care? Why hadn't Jesus tried to get him out? Had his hard work, sacrifice and faith been in vain?

Finally one gloomy day, John called two of his friends and said, "Go ask Jesus if he's the one God promised or if we should keep looking" (see Luke 7:19; Matt. 11:2-11). It's notable that John's inner uncertainty did not shame him into silence. He asked a direct question and Jesus responded. Equally intriguing is that John's doubt did not lower him in Jesus' estimation. "Among those born of women there has not risen anyone greater," said Jesus (Luke 7:28).

It's not possible to have flawless trust 24 hours a day, 7 days a week, 52 weeks a year over an entire lifetime. All that trying will never produce perfect faith. Even the "greatest man born of a woman" (the same man who baptized Jesus only a few months before) needed reassurance from Christ. Jesus was patient with John's questions. He is understanding with our doubts and imperfection, too.

Stop *Shoulding* Yourself in the Foot

Most of us either try too hard or we quit trying. In both cases, we miss God.
LINDA DILLOW, *CALM MY ANXIOUS HEART* [6]

Upon high school graduation, I entered Moody Bible Institute in Chicago, Illinois. After overdoing and over-serving, resulting

in bouts of laryngitis and hives, I felt rather numb and wanted
to sit on the sidelines and recoup with God before I committed
to any extracurricular ministry activities. When I mentioned
this to an upper classmate mentor, she responded, "That's a
selfish attitude." Immediately, I felt the shame of being human,
feeling tired and requiring rest.

"Christians are routinely taught by example and word that
it is more important to be right . . . than it is to be Christlike,"
writes Karen Lee-Thorp, in *Waking Up from the Dream of a
Lifetime*, a group study for women.[7] Lee-Thorpe contends that
sometimes we, as committed Christians, are encouraged to be
hard on people (ourselves included) who we believe are wrong.
Sadly, we're often persuaded that we need to "hold feet to the
fire" in order to reach spiritual maturity and become better
Christians. Yet this approach may lead to over-trying, numbness and eventual spiritual burnout.

Perhaps you try hard, but can't meet your goal—or someone
else's—of obtaining daily spiritual perfection. You're just really
tired. All that trying has produced increased deadness and you
feel like giving up. You didn't plan this. Perhaps you neglected
your relief-time with God while keeping busy and trying to look
good. Maybe you're confused by unfair experiences or disappointed by the unloving action of others, especially after
attempting so hard to obey God and do everything just right.

"I remember that day my quiet time died. After gathering all my devotional props, I settled into a terrible emptiness. I needed God as I had never needed him before,
but my regimented prayers were puny containers for
my anguish."

Jan Johnson, *Enjoying the Presence of God*[8]

If you're feeling numb and wondering where Jesus is, remember Jesus' response to Cousin John's uncertainty and questions. He welcomes your honest inquiries and isn't put off by your numbness or pain, even though you're worried others might be. It doesn't matter what others think right now. You can stop trying so hard to do and be what you cannot touch or feel—it's only dulling your soul, anyway.

Recently, I read these relief-inspiring words by Elizabeth Prentiss: "When your hearts will not fly, let them go, and if they will neither fly nor go, be sorry for them and be patient with them, and take them to Christ as you would carry your little lame child to a tender-hearted, skillful surgeon. Does the surgeon, in such a care, upbraid the child for being lame?"[9] Take your numbed, tired heart to God. He sees your pain and does not reprimand. You don't have to be perfectly spiritual to come to Jesus. He is the skillful surgeon and His bedside manner includes compassion and gentleness. He'll carry you when you're too numb to walk, teach you how to use crutches when you get strong enough and encourage you until the healing is complete.

He heals the brokenhearted (Ps. 147:3).

Lord Jesus,
How can I expect to prove
my spiritual competency if I cease striving?
Yet I'm tired and numb from trying to prove my faith.
Help me. I'm confused.
Hold me. I'm scared.
My soul longs to sing again.
Please show me how.

CHAPTER 15

I Double Dare You!

That I may know Him.

Philippians 3:10, *NKJV*

I had a deeply imbedded desire that I held carefully in my heart. Sometimes I felt alone with this longing. (Perhaps because as an introvert I didn't verbalize my dreams much, if at all.) My desire? To know God—to *really* know Him.

I wondered how to pursue my desire when, as a young mother, I felt so tired. *Physically* tired from running after a spirited three-year-old girl during the day and waking up six to seven times each night with a darling but fussy baby boy with chronic ear infections. *Emotionally* wiped-out from dealing with people's demands and my church commitments as a pastor's wife, Sunday School teacher and children's choir director. *Spiritually* drained from giving out without much input, and *relationally* starved due to lack of time and energy for cultivating friendships. (I ran a part-time daycare in my home plus another small business.) About that same time, I began writing a children's book.[1] I so enjoyed all these blessings, yet what I really wanted was to fulfill my desire. (And I wanted to do it *right*—whatever that meant!)

"Help, Lord," I whispered.

God heard and moved mountains just for me. Well, not exactly and not immediately, but several years later, He moved our family *through* the mountains from Visalia, California, to Shawnee Mission, Kansas. And up from my deeply planted desire grew a tiny sprout. God seemed to say, "See this seedling, Joan? Its name is *Prayer*. Nourish it. Water it. Watch it grow. This is the way to know Me."

Ever since I could remember, prayer had played a vital role in my life. Yet I felt God inviting me to a new level of intimacy with Him—and the possibility excited and challenged me. Mother Teresa once said, "Prayer enlarges the heart until it is capable of containing God's gift of Himself."[2] This is exactly the invitation I felt God was offering.

"There is a place within each one of us that is spiritual in nature . . . Here God's Spirit dwells with our spirit, and here our truest desires make themselves known. From this place we cry out to God for deeper union with him and with others."

Ruth Haley Barton, *Sacred Rhythms*[3]

Setting the alarm a few minutes earlier than usual, I planned to spend those moments alone with God. I purchased a small yellow notepad and wrote the word "Prayer" at the top of the first page. On the notepad, I listed my family's names. Under each name I wrote one or two words describing my prayer request for that person.

My prayer time didn't always work the way I envisioned it would. Sometimes (well, quite often) the children awakened before my alarm sounded. Surprisingly, I learned to have my alone times with them running circles around my chair. What happened during these imperfect God-meetings astonished me. After praying for a specific person or situation, God brought to my memory instances that demonstrated how He was answering. I jotted down the evidence and then to the list added other names: friends, pastors, clients and neighbors, organizations and ministries, government workers, the author of the book I was reading, and an unidentified person I chatted with at the store.

Scribbling God's answers up and down and around the margins and edges of each page, I realized I didn't have enough space. It got messy, so I bought a three-ring binder of notebook paper. I drew a straight line down the middle of the page. On the first line of the left column on the first page, I wrote the number "1" and a simple prayer. I skipped a line and numbered it "2" and jotted another short prayer. Within the next several months, I filled the left column of numerous pages with uncomplicated, heart-felt prayers.

I faced a blank space next to each written prayer, planning to fill this right column with God's answers. I watched and waited. Soon the right side overflowed with phrases of praise. The written initials *TY* became a code for the words "Thank You, Lord."

Many days I wrote no prayers, simply skimming a few existing ones, praying as I read. I didn't pray each prayer every day; there were too many and I didn't have much discretionary time. Some days were more inspiring than others. But it didn't matter, because my heavenly Father and I were spending time together. I talked to Him, listened and waited expectantly, and sensed His Spirit engaging with my spirit. God responded, recalling to my mind (and heart) His involvement in my daily circumstances and revealing Himself through His Word, creation and life. I experienced firsthand what the writer of Romans described: "The Spirit Himself bears witness with our spirit that we are children of God" (8:16, *NKJV*).

As months became years, I decided to date each prayer and answer. Even now I sometimes skim prayer journals of prior years and write the familiar initials *TY* with a current date and short update. I have noticed that God's answers don't always arrive as I envision they will. Consequently, I've altered the way I view answered and unanswered prayer. I now look for God's *responses,* not merely His answers. He responds with creativity. Sometimes He seems to say, "I think it'd be best to wait" or "Let's view this another way." Occasionally He prompts me to alter the request or gently prods me to dig deeper and ask, "Joan, what do you really want?" At times He just says, "I have a better idea."

A Better Idea

Several years ago, we decided to buy a place after renting an apartment for four years. We prayed, researched, found a condo we loved, made an offer they accepted and set a closing date. On September 11, 2001, we learned that the county had mistakenly listed the condo as VA-approved (Richard is an Army veteran) when it was not. We lost our dream place on a golf course.

We waited awhile and started looking again. In order to make the best investment, we decided to buy in a new condo development before they broke ground. "In three months, you'll move in," the salesman said.

Three months became five. "God, please protect us. If this is our house, work it out. If not, let us know," I prayed. Five months became seven, then nine. Often we walked through our unfinished condo, took measurements, dreamed and planned. We remained patient with the builder's "reasons." Almost one year later, the company went bankrupt. Disappointed and tired, we vowed to stay in the apartment.

A few days later, we heard of a house that had fallen out of escrow and was reduced for quick sale in a development we loved, but wasn't VA-approved. God surprised us with a financial windfall in the time since our last two disappointments, so we obtained a conventional loan, purchased that house on the day we saw it and moved in three weeks later.

For over four years, we've awakened each morning in this home on a golf course with adequate square footage to accommodate babysitting the six grandchildren God's given us (a condo would have been so cramped!). We unceasingly thank God that He had a better idea for us and didn't answer our prayer exactly how we imagined He should.

"Has God trusted you with a silence—a silence that is big with meaning? God's silences are His answers. Just think of those days of absolute silence in the home at Bethany [when Jesus did not come at Mary and Martha's request, and Lazarus died]. . . . His silence is the sign that He is bringing you into an even more wonderful understanding of Himself."

Oswald Chambers, *My Utmost for His Highest*[4]

No matter how quickly or slowly time passes without an obvious prayer response, I now believe God doesn't waste genuine prayers. Sometimes in my prayer notebook, I draw an X through a left-column prayer that no longer remains current. Yet I never X-out the right column because praises yield reasons to trust God for new situations. Above all, the Spirit reveals the personality and heart of God connecting me to my initial desire: *to know God intimately.*

So much has happened since I compiled that first prayer journal.[5] On occasion, God seemed silent—and I think He was, intentionally. Perhaps He tried to communicate with me, but something or someone else drowned out His words. I'm not surprised by this, for the process of growing and becoming comfortable in God's constant presence is similar to the process of growing through toddler-hood, childhood and adolescence: It's done awkwardly by trial and error, a messy process for imperfect children of God. Yet God gently pushes past our human logic and queries with His still voice, saying, "Pray anyway, always" (see 1 Thess. 5:17).

What Did Jesus Pray?

Jesus did many other things as well.
If every one of them were written down,
I suppose that even the whole world
would not have room for the books that
would be written.
JOHN 21:25

God understands how hard it is to live in this chaotic world and fit everything into our overcrowded schedules. He sent His Son to Earth to accomplish the greatest mission ever given to anyone (see Eph. 3:11-12). Like us, Jesus had only 24 hours each day. Strangers *and* close associates clamored for Jesus' time and attention. During His three-year ministry, He worked, taught, healed, blessed, traveled, ate, slept, advised and planned while training a team of 12 improbable leaders and encountering daily hostility. One might think Jesus didn't have time to pray, yet Jesus often withdrew to secluded places and prayed (see Luke 5:16).

I've often wondered what Jesus prayed. Did He discuss His schedule? Tell God how much He missed being in heaven? Praise God's virtues? Renew His commitment to His mission? Ask for strength to be human? Request a safe place to sleep? Pray for those who mocked Him? Or simply sit or kneel in His Father's presence?

A recorded statement gives clues about Jesus' prayers: "Peter, Satan asked to sift you like wheat," said Jesus. "I've prayed your faith won't fail. Yet I know you'll struggle. After you reconnect to Me, reach out to help others" (see Luke 22:32). Jesus saw Peter's need and prayed for him though He knew Peter would temporarily mess up. Even after Peter's denial became public (see Luke 22:54-62), Jesus trusted Peter enough to give him a significant life mission: to nurture other Christians (see John 21:15-19). Perhaps Jesus prays for you and me in a similar way.

Imperfectly Creative Times with God

A quiet time trains us to focus and to hear God—
skills necessary to enjoy God's presence.
JAN JOHNSON, *ENJOYING THE PRESENCE OF GOD* [6]

We enrich our human relationships when we spend time with our loved ones. We don't say exactly the same words or do the same activities each time we meet. By eating, sharing, playing, working, planning, crying or questioning together, we grow to know and appreciate one another. Likewise, our friendship with the triune God (Father, Son and Spirit) deepens when we move past the religious ruts and enjoy Him expansively (see John 15:15). I think God longs for us to want to be with Him so much that we become creative with our desire. Maybe one of the following suggestions will stimulate your creative juices and give you permission to relax and enrich your time with God.

A Prayer Diary

Connecting with God on paper about what's stirring in my heart and listening for His sometimes subtle responses is one way I come to know Him better. I don't always use the two-columned prayer journal. Sometimes I intersperse my regular journal with spontaneous notes to the Lord—or skip it for weeks at a time. I do realize journaling appeals more to certain temperaments than others.[7] It's fine if it doesn't sound like fun for you or if it doesn't fit your life right now. There are other ways to connect with God.

Praying Without Pencil, Rules or Strategies

I've worked at being spontaneous, yet I know others do it effortlessly. What a gift! Approaching God immediately and directly means in part that you ease off a need to say just the right words at the perfect time. It means coming to Him *before* you have your message all figured out. You're free to express childlike wonder without fearing that He might chide you for not being deep enough. It may mean sharing your delight in the season's first flower or horror at abuse portrayed on television. God's big enough for it all: the current Middle East crisis, the birth of a new baby or new believer, floods in the Midwest and my traffic jam. I don't get it! But that's okay, because I am me and God is God and sometimes that's the only thing that makes any sense.

Whether we experience a grateful heart, express simple pleasure at God's creation, silently admit confusion or intentionally ask God for help, we are praying. These serendipitous expressions offered internally or aloud show the amazing evidence of God's Holy Spirit within us. Value these prayers. God does. Remember:

It's your heart, not the dictionary, that gives meaning to your words (Matt. 12:34, *THE MESSAGE*).

Praying God's Word

Author and theologian Tony Jones writes, "Because [the Bible is] God-breathed, it has the ability to breathe God's Spirit into us."[8] For hundreds of years, Christians have turned Scripture into personal prayer. (When I got the idea over 15 years ago to pray God's Word, I thought I had a fresh approach. Ha!) Praying the Bible in a thoughtful, methodical way is called *lectio divina*, and although it sounds intimidating, it really isn't.

For example, I often read, meditate, contemplate and pray the words of Ephesians 1:17-19 for myself, a loved one or an associate: *Father, I ask You in Jesus' Name, to give [Rich, Adam, Dad] the Spirit of wisdom and insight so that he'll know You better. I pray also that the eyes of his heart may be enlightened to know the hope to which You've called us, the riches of Your glorious inheritance among us, and the incomparably great power that You give to all who believe in You.* You can pray this way in the silence of your heart or in a group.

Groaning Prayer

David (the shepherd-turned-king) expressed many negative, uncomfortable, even depressed thoughts and feelings in his recorded prayers to God. We need not perk up our down moods or deny our sadness and disappointment before we talk with God. The Old Testament book of Lamentations is filled with grief-laced prayers, yet God did not want it left out of the Bible. Neither did He censor David's mourn-filled songs.

> We do not know what we ought to pray for, but the Spirit himself intercedes for us with groans that words cannot express (Rom. 8:26).

God does not run away, as others may, when our words turn into groans. If you're experiencing loss, pain or distress right now, perhaps you'd like to use one of David's psalms as a backdrop during your moments with God. Any of the following psalms may help you verbalize your emotions: Psalms 6, 9–10, 25, 26, 27, 28, 31, 39, 40, 42–43, 55, 56, 57, 61, 70, 71, 77, 102, 120 and 139. You might wish to use a paraphrase such as *The Message Remix* or *The Living Bible* so that the depth of the psalmists' emotions come through clearly to you.

Praying the Neighborhood

During my recovery from burnout, I took long walks around the neighborhood, truly wondering if I'd ever think rationally or feel real again. Then one day as I walked past a new friend's house, a fresh idea blossomed: *I'll pray for her and her family.* To my surprise, the words I prayed made sense. *Lord, bring Your healing love and salvation to this house. Draw my friend's husband to You. Protect the two young boys. Do Your work.* Each day when their red house came into view, I visualized lifting this family to God.[9]

Soon I began praying for people I'd never met who lived in other houses I passed. I prayed for the confused and those with a secret longing to know God, that they would have the courage to attend a local church or Bible study—that they'd be drawn to His Son (see John 12:32). While walking, I grew to know God more intimately and identify with His deep compassion for people.

You might adapt the neighborhood prayer into a slightly different creative prayer venture. Over several months, one teen prayed through her school yearbook. Viewing each photo, she prayed for that peer by name. Another idea: Pray for those in your community phonebook or church directory.

> Absolutely everything, ranging from small to large, as you make it a part of your believing prayer, gets included as you lay hold of God (Matt. 21:22, *THE MESSAGE*).

Alphabet Prayers

I admit it, I don't like to stop whatever important thing I'm doing to take my daily building-better-bones walks. Once I push myself out the door, however, I do appreciate that unapologetically blue Arizona sky (like no other anywhere, but I'm biased!). During these walks, I talk with God or listen to praise music. Sometimes I pray versions of the alphabet prayer. (Mothers and grandmothers, you might include your children as you walk together or push the stroller to the park.)

1. *Alphabet Thanksgiving.* Name what you're grateful for starting with *A* and proceeding through *Z*. Example: Father, thank You for the:

   A. Air we breathe.
   B. Bird I just saw.
   C. Clouds.
   D. Duck in the pond.
   E. Evergreen trees.
   F. Flowers. And so on, through the entire alphabet if you have time.

2. *Alphabet Scripture Prayers.* Think of Bible verses, phrases or even Scripture songs you've learned lately and turn them into prayers. Example: Lord, your Word says, "**A**bide in me" (John 15:4); "**B**elieve in the Lord Jesus" (Acts 16:31); "**C**reate in me a clean heart" (Ps. 51:10) and "He **C**ares for you" (1 Pet. 5:7). (Remember, there's no perfect way to do this!)

3. *Alphabet Praises.* My favorite adaptation of this idea is to praise God for His attributes and characteristics. Example: Lord God, I praise You because You are:

   A. Awesome
   B. Blessed, Beautiful, Big
   C. Caring, Compassionate, Cool

D. Delightful, Defender, Deliverer
E. Excellent, Everlasting
F. Forgiving, Father, Forever, Freedom-Giver

No matter which you choose, be gentle with yourself and your children. If you can't think of anything for a letter, skip it and move on. If you don't know the verse's exact wording, paraphrase. Just have fun and let your mind and soul be bathed with God's words and gifts.

Prayer Relief in an Imperfect World

The night before Jesus announced the names of His discipleship team, He prayed all night (see Luke 6:12-16). Jesus chose the men carefully. After all, what they said and how they behaved reflected on His ministry. He spent hours preparing them. Yet even after all of that prayer, care, investment and training, Judas, one of those He chose to carry on His work, betrayed Him.

Even though we pray fervently—the best we can with what we know—things don't always turn out the way we plan. Our lives do not always look perfect or feel great. We may wonder what we missed or how we could have prayed more effectively. Please let yourself off the false-guilt hook. Not all prayer methods or tools will feel appealing, natural or authentic to you. You are a distinctive woman of God, designed with unique preferences. God understands. You do not need to be who you are not.

For example's sake, let's visualize the following scenario: Your best friend (an introvert) prefers working alone, writing out her prayers, learning from intense research and inductive study. But you (an extrovert) prefer praying and interacting with friends, trying new ideas with spontaneous and less structured knowledge-gathering. While undoubtedly you will be enriched by learning through organized study and thinking exercises and your friend will find additional meaning by sharing her emotions and allowing spontaneous interchange, these will never be the first choices for either of you.

"If Extroverted types are surrounded by silent environments, attend meetings or services with long pauses for meditation, or are required to sit still or focus on one idea for too long, they might conclude that they struggle spiritually," write the authors of *Soultypes: Matching Your Personality and Spiritual Path*. Conversely, "if Introverted types spend too much time in group discussion, participating in active learning experiences or are asked to share deep thoughts too freely they might mistakenly conclude that they struggle spiritually."[10] By granting ourselves and others space and grace, we actually reduce frustration and potential spiritual burnout and encourage deeper connectedness with God.

"We all come to prayer with a tangled mass of motives—altruistic and selfish, merciful and hateful, loving and bitter. . . . But what I have come to see is that God is big enough to receive us with all our mixture. We do not have to be bright, or pure or filled with faith, or anything. That is what grace means, and not only are we saved by grace, we live by it as well. And we pray by it."

Richard J. Foster, *Prayer: Finding the Heart's True Home*[11]

I offer you a challenge: Choose just one of the prayer methods mentioned in this chapter and commit to doing it consistently for only two weeks. (Hint: It doesn't need to be every day!) Whatever you choose, remember that none of us understands or prays perfectly at all times. We simply cannot figure out all things. Personal insight usually comes slowly. By striving to gain more and more and more, we merely tighten the blindfold on ourselves. So let's relax. Practicing patience with our spiritual prayer process is a relief-filled way to live.

What prayer focus will you enjoy with God during the next few days? Oops! Some of you chose two! I dare you to choose *only one* and practice it imperfectly. No, I double dare you! What do you say?

Relief Reminder

Before reading the next section, "The Promise of Relief: The Smile of Imperfection," take a break and play through the Relief Guide for Imperfect Faith, Prayer and Spirituality. You may do it alone or invite someone to join you.

The Relief of Imperfect Faith, Prayer and Spirituality

After reading chapters 14 and 15, I invite you to respond to the following questions and exercises in your Relief Journal. Remember that you always have the option to respond *Yes, No, Renegotiate* or *Later*.

1. With which story or illustration in chapters 14 and 15 do you identify? How?

2. "God longs for us to want to be with Him so much that we become creative with our desire." What are some ways you can slow down and just *be* with God?

3. The Bible gives guidelines for effective prayer, yet not all prayer and Bible study methods appeal to everyone. God created us with different preferences and temperaments. How does this offer you relief?

4. To help you determine your temperament tendency, circle the words/phrases in the columns on the following page that describe what you prefer to do. Then place an X on the arrowed line between the words/phrases at the point where you believe you register on the continuum between "extrovert" and "introvert." (We all can enjoy any of these activities at specific times, but usually not with equal confidence. Mark what you would *prefer* to do.)

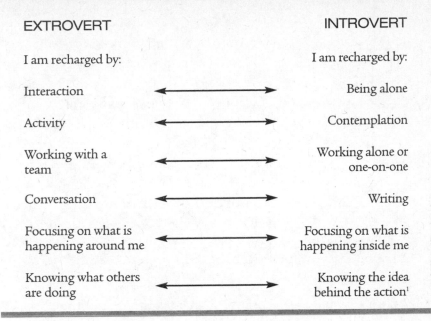

EXTROVERT		INTROVERT
I am recharged by:		I am recharged by:
Interaction	⟷	Being alone
Activity	⟷	Contemplation
Working with a team	⟷	Working alone or one-on-one
Conversation	⟷	Writing
Focusing on what is happening around me	⟷	Focusing on what is happening inside me
Knowing what others are doing	⟷	Knowing the idea behind the action[1]

5. Read the following poem and respond to the question "What do you need?"

> Some of us need to stop thinking and do,
>   while others need to stop doing and think.
> Some need to stop asking and give, though
>   others need to cease giving and ask.
> Some of us need to stop crying and smile,
>   yet others need to stop smiling and cry.
> Some need to stop confronting and give in,
>   while others need to quit compromising and confront.
> Some of us need to stop waiting and run,
>   Though others need to stop running and wait.
> Some need to practice discipline and organize,
>   yet others need to cease structuring themselves into a
>   box and relax.
> God is big enough to help us all. What do you need?

6. What relaxed prayer focus will you enjoy during the next few weeks? (*Pssst!* If you're having a tricky time deciding between two good choices, consider a quirky tool called the Flipped Coin Exercise. Because both choices are reasonable and beneficial and it really doesn't matter which one is just right, flip a coin. When you see which side it lands on, pay attention to how you feel about that choice. Are you happy it landed that way? A little disappointed? Now you know what you really wanted to do all along! You can also try this when you can't decide between two good possibilities in other areas of your life. It'll make you smile and give you a break from trying too hard to make it just right!)

Take a few minutes to pray and share your dreams, thoughts and feelings with God. Jot your prayer in your Relief Journal. Listen for God's response(s) and consider writing down what you think He's showing you right now.

We throw open our doors to God and discover at the same moment that he has already thrown open his door to us. We find ourselves standing where we always hoped we might stand—out in the wide open spaces of God's grace and glory, standing tall and shouting our praise (Rom. 5:1, *THE MESSAGE*).

Lord, thanks for opening Your arms to me
and ushering me out of my shame and
away from my trying-too-hard prison.
I know I'll never have perfect faith, but that's okay.
I love living in the freedom of Your love and grace.

The Promise of Relief:

The Smile of Imperfection

CHAPTER 16

Permission to Exhale

Let the smile of your face shine on us, LORD.
You have given me greater joy than those who
have abundant harvests of grain and wine.
I will lie down in peace and sleep, for you alone,
O LORD, will keep me safe.

Psalm 4:6-8, *NLT*

Although my biofeedback experience bombed (remember how I broke the machine?), my trips to the physical therapist weren't entirely a fiasco. The therapist taught me how to breathe.

I know, I know—everybody breathes, right? There wouldn't be very many people doing very much of anything if we didn't already know how to breathe.

But the truth is, most of us are shallow breathers. We don't inhale enough of the pure, energizing air our bodies and minds need, and we don't exhale all the stale, used-up air that's taking up space. The result is predictable: foggy thinking, depression and/or anxiety, racing heart, tired body, tense muscles, lack of focus, and on and on. This is how my therapist taught me to breathe:

Slowly breathe in through your nose (from your diaphragm, which is the muscle below your lungs that expands them for filling), hold for a moment and then breathe out through your mouth for several seconds. Then do it again and again.[1] At first I couldn't breathe in or out for more than a split second. It felt foreign. Sometimes it still does.

When solving a problem, meeting a deadline or living a normal day, I tend to hold my breath or breathe shallowly. I then remind myself to stop sucking it in and just let it out.

I remember the first time I discovered that the conscious act of breathing (the way the physical therapist taught) actually helped—it calmed me down and contributed to clearer thinking. (Big surprise.) I was on the freeway, driving across town to meet a colleague for lunch. I flowed with traffic for 30 minutes; then suddenly the driver in front of me flashed his brake lights and screeched to a halt. Every car did likewise and the freeway resembled the local used-car lot. (You've experienced this, I'm sure.)

"Great," I mumbled. "What's going on?" *Construction, lane closings, sports event, accident?* Trying hard to practice patience, I gritted my teeth and waited. *Okay, if it let's up in a few moments, I'll make it on time.* But we didn't budge. Nothing. *Bummer. I hate to be late. She'll think I forgot. It'll throw off her busy schedule. Mine, too. Makes me look unorganized. Oh, well . . . I tried. I left in enough time. Well, maybe not. I should have known.* I felt myself slipping down into the internal self-berating abyss. (The old adage, "Every morning is the dawn of a new error," came to mind.)

"Set me free from my prison, that I may praise your name."

Psalm 142:7

That's when I remembered. *Breathe, Joan. Try breathing.* I took in a long breath through my nose and let it out slowly through my mouth. Once. Twice. Again. Slower. Again. One minute. Two, three, four, five. That's when it happened: My defeated "Not again! Oh, well . . ." became a genuinely relaxed and smile-able "So what? Being late isn't the end of the world." I chuckled, even laughed. *Janet will understand.* By that time, I knew the stall was

due to a wreck up ahead. So I just waited and breathed—
repeatedly. (In case you wonder why I didn't call her on my cell
phone, I didn't have one. Only a beeper. Hey, this happened several years ago.) Finally, the accident was cleared away, traffic
moved and I took the next exit, turning into the restaurant
parking lot. I was *that* close to my destination the entire time.

I greeted my friend, sharing my "freeway" story and how I
coped, not with dour stress-streaked resignation, but with relief-
filled breathing. "Well, you've made my day, Joan," she said. "I'm
happy for you." Janet had been with me when my mind threatened to leave my body. When I was poised on the brink of a nervous breakdown, she gently talked me back and invited me to stay
with her that day so that she could keep an eye on me.

I believe God put Janet in my life to be a "stretcher bearer"
(see Luke 5:18-20). When I couldn't help myself, she was there.
I telephoned her when my hands shook. She listened and affirmed
my genuine desire to escape burnout and become the person
God designed me to be. When weeks turned to months and I still
felt nauseated and couldn't think straight, she waited patiently.
She didn't offer quick advice, quote Scripture verses or give reasons for my dilemma. She simply supported my recovery, though
she never mentioned the word. She took to heart Paul's words to
the Ephesians: "Be patient with each other, making allowance for
each other's faults because of your love" (4:2, *NLT*).

At times I think she was confused by my rambling and saddened by my pain, yet I never got the impression she felt responsible for my health. She left the responsibility with me and
expected God to work. You may need someone like this as you're
escaping the perfectionism trap—someone who accepts you
where you are and encourages you to move forward, trust God
more and fear less.

Trying too hard to make it just right—with symptoms like fixing, people-pleasing, controlling, over-doing, perfectionism and

playing God—produces anxiety, undue pressure and fear. Yet faith can progressively replace fear, bringing the smile of imperfection to your face and relief to your soul. The wise writer of Proverbs said, "Don't assume that you know it all. Run to God! . . . Your body will glow with health, your very bones will vibrate with life!" (3:7-8, *THE MESSAGE*). Sounds pretty good, right?

Courage to Jump

It isn't brave to do something that you're not afraid of.
But it's very brave to face up to something which
frightens you paralytic.
ROSAMUNDE PILCHER, *"A GIRL I USED TO KNOW"*[2]

I stood with my toes curled over the side of the boat, knees knocking. Everywhere I looked, I saw only water and sky. *What am I doing?* I won't even let the water from the shower splash on my face! How could I possibly think of jumping into the ocean? *I can't do this!* I stared down at the rolling waves and argued with myself. *No. Yes. No. Maybe.*

"The only thing that separates any one of us from excellence is fear, and the opposite of fear is faith. I am careful not to confuse excellence with perfection. Excellence I can reach for, perfection is God's business."

Michael J. Fox, actor, husband, father, Parkinson's patient

My husband reached from the water below; the instructor on the boat deck tapped my shoulder. I adjusted my life jacket, took a deep breath and jumped. Bright blue, pink and yellow fish greeted me. I wanted to shout, "I did it!" (I refrained, however—I didn't want to lose the mouthpiece that kept me breathing during this snorkeling venture!)

I grabbed my husband's hand and together we explored the lovely sights of God's underwater creation. I walked beyond my fear and experienced celebration and delight I never would have known had I not jumped into the ocean that frightened me.

Are your knees trembling as you stand with your toes curled over the edge of your life boat? Perhaps you look out and see only looming clouds of what-if questions. *What if I stop trying so hard? Release control? Lighten up? Will God still want to partner with me? Will I impact others' lives anymore?*

The Fear Game

With God's help I can jump over a wall. . . .
God is my protection. . . .
He makes me like a deer that does not stumble . . .
You support me with your right hand. . . .
You give me a better way to live.
PSALM 18:29-36, *NCV*

Brennan Manning, author of *Posers, Fakers, and Wannabes,* writes, "It breaks God's heart that we are afraid of him, afraid of life, afraid of each other, afraid of ourselves."[3] Maybe you play this *No-Yes-No-Yes-Maybe* game with yourself and secretly wonder what adventure or blessing you'll miss if your fear keeps you from jumping into your future with God. If you do, you're not alone. Carol Kent, well-known speaker and author of *Tame Your Fears,* lists several forms of perfectionistic fear that disturb a woman's sense of well-being and hope-filled anticipation.[4] These include:

- Fear of what hasn't happened yet. *What if I lose my job? What if the terrorists strike again? What if the plane crashes and our kids become orphans? What if I get cancer?*

- Fear of revealing myself or losing control. *What if they discover I never finished college? Had an abortion? What if getting married robs my individuality?*

- Fear of abandonment, disapproval or rejection. *What if I never get married? What if my husband leaves? Dies? What if I don't fit in? Am I too fat? What if they don't like me?*

- Fear of facing reality. *What if they knew how much debt we have? What if my husband is cheating on me? What if I admit to burnout? What if my daughter remains homeless and never works?*

- Fear of losing faith or intimacy with God. *What if God's mad at me? What if I miss God's calling? What if I change and my family doesn't like me anymore?*

- Fear of poor choices or being trapped. *What if I'm stuck in this job forever? My husband never changes? I never lose weight? I can't quit throwing up?*

- Fear of failure or success. *What if accepting this promotion is bad for the kids? What if I get too busy? Can't keep up? Get a divorce? Lose my job? Fail again?*

One-Half the Work

Cast all your anxiety on him because he cares for you.
1 PETER 5:7

Perfectionistic fear can chain you to the status quo and keep you from becoming who you want to be and doing what you believe God called you to do. Our what-if fears, like those above, relate to our tomorrows, whether in 5 or 10 years, next month, next week or one minute from now.

Paul, the former CAO (Chief Abusement Officer) of all Early Christians, and the author of Romans, writes, "For I am convinced that neither death nor life, neither angels nor demons, neither the present nor the future, nor any powers, neither height nor depth, nor anything else in all creation, will be able to separate us from the love of God that is in Christ Jesus our Lord" (Rom. 8:38-39). God's grace-filled love and protection cover all our perfectionistic fears about tomorrow. I get excited every time I read Paul's assuring words that no person, place or thing can ever come between us and God's love.

1. Death cannot. Whether I drown in the ocean I fear, at the hands of terrorists, from cancer or natural causes, the result is the same: I see Jesus. And if the dying itself seems more than I can emotionally or physically bear (that's what concerns me), Christ's Spirit promises to help me in and through the pain (see John 14:16-17).

2. Nothing inside—worries, negative thoughts, depression, disappointment, anxiety—or outside—runaway kids, education or lack of it, declining health, in-laws, difficult marriage, singleness—can separate you and me from God's love (see Mark 6:5).

3. No one in authority can come between God and us. No matter what happens with our political leaders or government, or how church leadership disappoints and saddens us, God's love will never betray us.

4. Nothing yet to come—the aging process, parents' illness and death, empty nest, all that's beyond our influence and control, our own future plans—can keep God from loving us.

5. Nowhere you and I fly, drive, sail or walk can keep us from God.

Then, as if he hadn't emphasized his point strongly enough, Paul adds, "I am persuaded beyond any doubt that absolutely nothing can separate me from God's pure and unconditional love, which is mine (and yours) because Jesus—the God-Man—made this incredible reality possible" (see Rom. 8:39).

Sometimes faith seems like the ultimate paradox: I give up what I long for; I let go in order to find what is missing. Letting go means trusting that the decision to surrender is okay, that the process will be worthwhile, that God is in complete control of the result. Faith means loosening my grip on people, things, jobs, organizations and circumstances. Faith believes that God is in charge, that He can and will do what I cannot see or figure out.

Allison MacMurtrie, a single mother of two and a small-business owner, found out that God works even in the worst of circumstances:

It's so unfair! How could this happen? It hurts so much. I just don't get it. I cried. I stopped. Then started again. I simply couldn't believe this was happening to me. Divorce? Who would have thought?

What am I going to do? I'm so angry. Unhappy. So afraid. How will we make it? I can't think. What shall I say to the girls? Will they be okay? Will I? I had read all the books. Studied the Bible. Everyone said there was an ideal (godly) way to do marriage. I thought I did it. I followed the biblical directives. I prayed for my husband and our marriage all those years. I did the right things. *If I do A and B, then C will happen.* It didn't. What happened? I was sure I did it the right way. I thought I did.

My pain cut so deep, I didn't think I'd ever smile again. It did take awhile. It's been several years, but I've found that God is quite creative. He uses many different circumstances and ways to produce health, good character and growth in His willing children. Books, preachers and Bible teachers may tell me there is one way God works—and many times that one way is the method He used in their lives—but truthfully, sometimes God operates in different ways. There doesn't seem to be a perfect way, except to trust Him even when your heart breaks. And even the trusting doesn't come simply. What I know now: God always has the best idea.

Someone recently asked me, "What's the benefit to believing this way now?" I thought about it for only a moment.

"Well, it's one-half the work. And a whole lot lighter," I said. "I was spinning my wheels before. So now I've stopped trying so hard to figure it all out and have the exact formula and solution to every hurt or problem.

"In fact, here's an exercise that helps me. I have a mental shelf marked for God. I take all my what-if and how-come and why questions and envision myself setting them on God's shelf. I *so* want to fix things. *What if I'd done it differently?* I can ask that over and over, but it just makes me tired and increases my anxiety. When I set what isn't mine to control on the mental shelf marked for God, I stop working too hard. God is better than I am at organizing it all. I still work hard, but not at God's job. I work hard at what's my own responsibility. As I said, I feel a whole lot lighter now."

It occurs to me that breathing comes easier when my fear gives way to faith. It's like God granting me permission to exhale.

Just today I had this give-and-take prayer conversation with my
Lord. (He started it!)

God: Joan, I love you.

Joan: That's nice. Thank You.

God: *Joan*, I love you. I *love* you. *I* love you. I love *you*. And
Joan, I'm proud of you.

Joan: Really?

God: Yes. Let Me love you. Take a breather from analyzing.

Joan: I know You think about me, Lord.[5] But do You
value me?

God: Yes, of course. Why else would I have sent My only
Son to redeem you?

Joan: But, Lord, are You pleased with what I'm doing?
I don't want to be number one; I just want to do and
be what You've planned for me.[6] Please show me.

God: I love you, Joan. My love is full of respect.

Joan: Yes, I would think so, for You love and respect the
dignity of all. I guess what I'm wondering is: Do You
love me with my uniqueness? Is that a very human
thing to ask?

God: Certainly, it is. But that is what you are—completely
human. One day you'll be with Me in heaven in My
home and then you'll not be "human." But now you are.

Joan: Still, I wonder if You're satisfied with me. But I'll
leave it for now. *Let it go.*

God: Okay, Joan. I love you. Is that enough?

Joan: On one hand, yes. On the other hand . . . well, actually that's yes, too! I'd just like to have more words or
enlightenment around Your *love*. You understand that,
don't You, Lord?

God: Yes. I made you the intensely thinking person you
are. So I know. (Pause.) Joan . . .

Joan: What?

God: (Pause.)

Joan: Yes? I'm listening.

God: (Silence.)

Joan: You're smiling, aren't You, Lord? Smiling at me—
and with me. Singing over me. (Pause.) Lord?

God: Just bask in My love, Joan. You don't have to try so
hard. Relax in My love and acceptance. I've done the
work. Jesus won your freedom. Now live, breathe,
enjoy.

Joan: (Smile.)

The LORD your God is with you . . . He will take great
delight in you, he will quiet you with his love, he will
rejoice over you with singing (Zeph. 3:17).

CHAPTER 17

Trading Exhausting Expectations for Imperfect Joy

I took a break from working in the office and I headed for the park. On a whim (I'm still learning to be more spontaneous), I decided to swing on the swing set. At first, pumping my legs took more energy than I thought it would. My knees hurt while I worked to get started, but once I pushed past the difficult stage, I closed my eyes and soared through the air. I glided for a while.

Then I realized: *This is what it's like to initiate change in my life.* It's hard work at first. I pump and pump just to get my "swing" activated, yet once I'm moving toward spiritual, mental, emotional or even physical transformation, the effort is always worthwhile. Occasionally I can even stop pumping to glide, but in order to keep swinging toward change, I need to stay committed to the basic work of pumping.

It takes daily practice to (1) stay aware of thinking that keeps us stuck in the trying-too-hard mode, and (2) replace those self-defeating thoughts with God's truth, current reality and positive action. It's unfamiliar, uncomfortable and often scary. When I tremble at the thought of changing my familiar yet exhausting habits, God promises to guide me and never leave. I carry this assurance in my heart, praying, journaling and breathing these words in Isaiah 42:16: "Along unfamiliar paths I will guide them; I will turn the darkness into light before them and make the rough places smooth. . . . I will not forsake them."

This Ongoing Adventure

Do your own work. Don't stare at the clouds. Get on with your life.
ECCLESIASTES 11:4, *THE MESSAGE*

Sometimes I get so drained trying to be the ideal wife, mother, friend, writer, daughter, sister, business owner, manager, speaker, teacher and Christian woman (that's the most confusing one at times) that I just want to step down from my regular life, go away to figure "it" out, and return all fixed and safe for the future. But as Sandy Richardson and Susan Wilsie Govier, authors of *Soul Hunger*, remind me, "Safety doesn't come from having all my ducks in a row."[1]

You'd think after all this time, I'd have the perfect (oops!) routine all formed, wrapped in a neat little package, and ready to open and use at a moment's notice. It isn't like that. While I do have tools that help, I don't have it (or me) all figured out. (Shock!) I still have to be persistent, committed and deliberate about maintaining balance (which is about making choices, saying yes to some things and no to others)[2] and taking current action steps to experience the relief of imperfection.

I wish I could guarantee that reading through this book will make everything better and you'll never need to address the trying-too-hard dilemma again. But the truth is that it's an ongoing adventure. The good news? It's worth the intentional "pumping of your swing." In our book, *The Intentional Woman*, Carol Travilla and I wrote:

Processing Life—with the good, painful, and disappointing—is an annoyingly slow procedure sometimes. Although the process is always worthwhile, sometimes it takes me to frightening places where I feel unfamiliar emotions and think uncomfortable thoughts. It takes courage to move beyond conditioned attitudes and behavior.[3]

I'm different than I used to be. Free-er. Less rigid with myself and others. It doesn't matter as much if something isn't explained just right or folded correctly. I'm more willing to ask for what I need. (Though this is still hard for me at times.) I don't feel as responsible for my husband's happiness and satisfaction with life. I laugh more readily. And because of all this, I'm a grateful woman. I truly am. Yet I'm certainly not perfect— and it's in admitting and accepting this that I find such relief! I identify with Katie Brazelton, author and founder of Pathway to Purpose Ministry, who wrote, "As I left behind my unreachable Utopia and entered the real world of laughable flaws, I experienced a freedom I did not expect."[4]

Mercy to You *and* Me

Take care of yourself . . . make the most of what God gives,
both the bounty and the capacity to enjoy it,
accepting what's given and delighting in the work.
It's God's gift! God deals out joy in the present, the now.
ECCLESIASTES 5:18-20, *THE MESSAGE*

Several years ago as I casually leafed through a stack of periodicals, I read some words that made a profound impression on me: "How we are with ourselves is exactly how we are with others. To the degree that we are gentle with ourselves, we are gentle with others. To the degree that we forgive ourselves, we forgive others. And to the degree that we love ourselves, we love others."[5] I jotted this quote by seminar leader and author Louisa Rogers in my journal.

Underneath, I wrote, "Perhaps this is the way to be less picky." I had prayed that God would show me how to be less exacting in my silent attitude toward other people, organizations and life's imperfections. Soon I noticed within me a growing tolerance toward those who looked, thought or behaved differently than I. Also, I was nicer to myself, refusing to be my own slave driver. Yet I accomplished even more than usual. Such a paradox. Imagine relaxed attitudes producing greater effectiveness and joy!

Recently during a coaching call, a client chided herself for, well, just about everything. She was *on a roll*. She said, "I guess my perfectionism is out of control. But I don't get it, because now my family tells me I try to control them. It's confusing—they can't give examples of when I do it. I'm between a rock and a hard place here." She squabbled with her husband over the weekend. Her sister's addictions flared. Personal health problems had escalated and doctors weren't helping much. Her stepdaughter's wedding plans loomed large. She wondered about her housekeeping and she felt disappointed in her recent business endeavors. Life's imperfection slapped her in the face and she blamed herself. "I should do this better," she concluded.

"When you allow the Lord to fill your heart with his boundless love, it shows on the outside. . . . It's an inside-out job. . . . People will think you've had a facelift, when in fact you've had a faith-lift!"

Liz Curtis Higgs, *Reflecting His Image*[6]

We discussed Louisa Rogers's quote about "how we are with ourselves is exactly how we are with others." She jotted the entire quote on several sticky notes and stuck them where she'd see them often (bathroom mirror, computer, journal, steering wheel). Throughout the day, she was reminded to befriend and support herself. Her shoulders relaxed and her stomach settled down. She talked to her husband and even had some fun. After sharing all this during our next call, she said, "I simply gave myself a break, just as I'd do for any other good friend."

By practicing Jesus' gentle but firm teaching of love and forgiveness with ourselves first, we're released from our self-preoccupation, such as *Am I doing this wrong? Do I look okay? Is he mad at me? I should be better.* We are free to extend mercy to others. In chapter 2, we noticed that Jesus' words "Be perfect" (Matt. 5:48) and "Be merciful" (Luke 6:36) encourage us to grow from the inside out, becoming complete in Him. This means that we don't merely focus on how we appear outwardly, but we mature and cherish what's happening internally. It's a heart thing.

Smile-able Truths

I've learned (well, I *am* learning) several relief-generating truths:

- *Some things don't matter!* Regardless of what we've been told by over-zealous pastors, teachers, grown-ups, friends, media or that inner bully, some issues are not direly important. Now I can say "It doesn't matter" with confidence when I find I'm trying too hard to make everything (or everyone, including me) just right.

  Paul's "It doesn't matter" statement about the less-than-excellent motives of other ministry leaders helps me release my need to make sure everybody gets it right: "Those leaders who seemed to be important did not change the Good News that I preach. (*It doesn't matter* to me if they were 'important' or not. To God everyone is the same)" (Gal. 2:6, *NCV*, emphasis added).

In another letter, he wrote, "In this new life, *it doesn't matter* if you are a Jew or a Gentile, circumcised or uncircumcised, barbaric, uncivilized, slave, or free. Christ is all that matters, and he lives in all of us" (Col. 3:11, *NLT*, emphasis added).

• *Take it easy!* A liberating question I sometimes ask myself is: *Because I'm going to do this [task, project, relationship] anyway, how can I make it easier or more fun?* On my desk next to my ergonomic keyboard sits my red EASY button.[7] When I need to lighten up, I press it and hear three little words recorded in a deep reassuring voice: *That was easy!* They remind me of Jesus' words: "Come here, Joan. Walk with me. I'm not trying to make it harder for you. I want to lighten your load" (my paraphrase of Matt. 11:29-30) and "Be easy on people; you'll find life a lot easier" (Luke 6:37, *THE MESSAGE*).

• *God's expectations are reasonable.* He patiently waits for me to become the trusting person He created me to be. To live, work, play and breathe into the personality, gifts, temperament, talents and womanhood He designed for me (see 1 Pet. 4:10).[8]

God's loving expectations and opportunities for you suit *you*. Mine suit me. God fashioned you and me to trust Him. We are most alive when we do. I'm fascinated by an explanation attributed to French philosopher Blaise Pascal: "There is a God-shaped vacuum in the heart of every [human] which cannot be filled by any created thing, but only by God, the Creator, made known through Jesus."

In order to exercise our trust, we take small—even imperfect—steps of faith: "It's impossible to please God apart from faith. And why? Because anyone who wants to approach God must believe both that he exists and that he cares enough to respond to those who seek him" (Heb. 11:6, *THE MESSAGE*).

- *People-pleasing negates spiritual growth.* Trying to be everything others want is an automatic crazy-maker. When you and I try to please people, we attempt to accomplish the impossible. How do we decide which human being to satisfy—a parent, colleague, boss, friend, pastor, sibling, spouse? Each of these individuals has a different image of us and often their expectations or plans for us are not consistent with our dreams, abilities, gifts or God-given calling. Let's recall a few more wise words of Paul: "We are not trying to please men but God, who tests our hearts" (1 Thess. 2:4).

- *Cooperating with our Creator to become the person He planned us to be releases us to freedom.* I've seen this happen in the lives of coaching clients, life plan partners, women in Intentional Woman classes, colleagues in the Network of IW Presenters *and* in the lives of friends and family members. God knows what is in our hearts. When He tests our hearts, He brings forth what is best in us. "It's in Christ that we find out who we are and what we are living for" (Eph. 1:11, *THE MESSAGE*).

Nicole Guelich, a wife, mother of three, runner and ministry volunteer, tells the following story of learning to smile in her imperfection:

I grew up trying to be perfect for God. I obeyed every rule, went to church and made what I thought were all the right choices. I consistently got As in school, because that was the best attainable result. When I had my first child, I rigidly maintained the ideal schedule for fear of losing control or making a mistake.

Later, friends asked how I managed to keep it all together so well (with twins and a preschooler, a husband and my regular life). They thought I looked perfect. They didn't know: *I hid the real me*. Unlike how they perceived me, I felt uptight, lonely, scared and overwhelmed with everything. Secretly, I longed for someone to rescue me.

A health scare a few years ago caused me to question my faith and who I had become. I knew Jesus as Savior, but felt an incredible void. *What am I missing?* I thought I was doing all God asked of me. Although I wasn't sure what, I wanted something else.

So I asked God to give me the desire to know Him authentically. Through much contemplation, prayer and the gentle guidance of a mentor, I gradually learned that God wasn't after flawless behavior, but my *heart*. One evening, my husband took the three kids out so that I could work around the house. Instead I knelt in my room and cried, "I give up, Lord. The way I'm doing life is not working. I surrender to You."

It felt like I took a running leap off a giant cliff into a vast unknown world. Frightened beyond belief, I fell into God's arms and experienced wholeness and freedom for the first time in my life. When perfectionistic anxiety threatens to pull me under again, I open my heart to God and He rescues me from my false self. I found what was missing and it isn't perfection. It's a relaxed, honest and intimate relationship with myself and God.

Isn't That a Relief?

Both good and bad things happen to everyone.
ECCLESIASTES 9:2, *NCV*

Tired after an extra-long work day, Richard and I decided to eat a simple dinner at home and watch a movie. Just for fun, we ate by candlelight. I rested while he cleaned up. It was a relaxing, recuperating evening. But then it happened: The phone rang. In the rush to answer it, we inadvertently knocked over a burning candle. It flew through the air, hitting the grand piano before it landed on the carpet. Huge globs of candle wax melted into the crevices of the piano and fibers of the plush carpet. We spent two hours cleaning up the mess. "How stupid!" he muttered. Previously I might have silently agreed.

This time I smiled inside. *I don't buy that anymore,* I thought. *It was an awkward situation, but no one or no thing is stupid because of it. Joy and fun can mix with mistakes and disappointment. A spilled candle mess need not wipe out the pleasure of the previous moments.*

We may have believed that everything is either wonderful and perfect or botched up and disastrous. But we're learning that imperfection and excellence (or "good enough") can co-exist. Life doesn't have to be perfect to be wonderful—and neither do our plans, work, relationships, emotions, bodies, churches, quiet moments or faith. Isn't that a relief? May we all learn to breathe deeply, trading our exhausting expectations for imperfect joy.

He puts a smile on my face. He's my God (Ps. 42:6, *THE MESSAGE*).

Come to me.
Get away with me and you'll recover your life.
I'll show you how to take a real rest.
Walk with me and work with me—watch how I do it.

Learn the unforced rhythms of grace.
I won't lay anything heavy or ill-fitting on you.
Keep company with me and you'll learn to
live freely and lightly.
(A message to you from Jesus, Matt. 11:28-30, *THE MESSAGE*)

Relief Reminder

Take your last relief break and play through the Relief Guide
for the Smile of Imperfection. You may wish to complete the
guide alone or ask a friend to join you. In either case, celebrate
your completion of *The Relief of Imperfection* with a smile-able
activity. (Some of you might choose to relax in a hammock or
take a nap, while others may decide to hike a hill or meet a
friend at the local coffee shop. Enjoy!)

The Smile of Imperfection

After reading chapters 16 and 17, "The Smile of Imperfection," please respond to the following questions and exercises in your Relief Journal.

1. Which story, illustration or smile-able truth in chapters 16 and 17 most impressed you? In what way?

2. Here's your opportunity to redo the *Relief of Imperfection* Awareness Wheel—after reading and playing through the book—and assess your current (as of today) expectations in six specific life areas. The six life areas you're measuring compare to the six "reliefs" in this book:

   - *Relationships and families*: friends, children, in-laws, grandchildren, extended family, spouse, dating

   - *Emotions, minds and bodies*: physical, emotional and mental well-being, health and body image issues, exercise, soul-care, journaling, education

   - *Life-work and service*: employment, career including full-time mother or homemaker, home-schooling, avocation/volunteer work

   - *Churches and culture*: church work, worship time, ministry, church leaders, missionary and charity affiliations, media, societal pressures, community/neighborhood

• *Dreams, plans and decisions*: current, future and former plans, choices, vision, purposes, opportunities

• *Faith, prayer and spirituality*: quiet times, prayer life, Bible study, relationship with God, spiritual formation

Remember: There's no perfect way to do your Wheel. It's for your awareness. Take a breath, have fun and share your discoveries!

A. In or near each wedge of the wheel on Figure 2, write one to three expectations you have for that area of your life. For example, "I should have a 45 minute Quiet Time each day" or "I'll always meet a deadline" or "Parents must always agree" or "I should never weigh above my ideal weight" or "I must never feel angry" or "My spouse should always listen to me" or "I need to cook a full meal every day."

B. With the center of the wheel as 0 and the outer edge as 10, rank your current sense of pressure or overwhelm in that area by drawing a curved line from one side of the wedge to the other. Ask, *What is my current sense of perfectionistic overwhelm in this area?*

C. Shade the area from the center to your curved line to help you visualize your current "relief of imperfection" level (see example). Where are you currently giving yourself relief-filled grace and space? In what areas are you sensing the pressure today?

D. What jumps out at you about your *Relief of Imperfection* Awareness Wheel today? Spend a few moments

Relief of Imperfection Awareness Wheel
Figure 1—Example

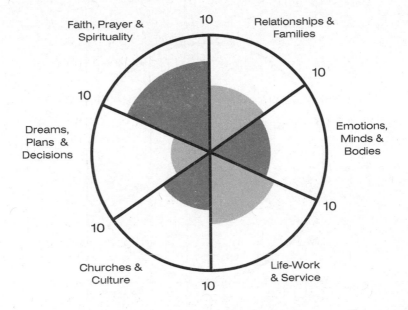

writing about how you're feeling right now and what you're discovering about yourself. Choose one area on your wheel where you would like to reduce your grade by one point and insert a little fresh air. What relief-producing action step will lower your score by one? When will you implement this step? Who will you tell about your decision?

3. Re-read Romans 8:38-39. Which assurance of God's love offers you the most comfort?

4. What have you learned about yourself, others, life or God while reading this book? What meaningful "relief of imperfection" have you experienced?

Relief of Imperfection Awareness Wheel
Figure 2—Your Turn

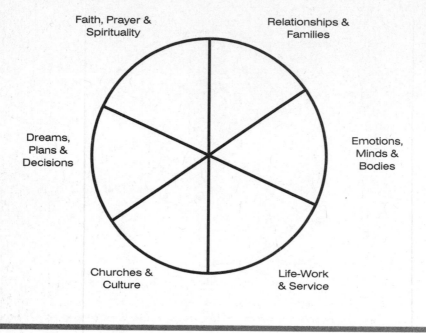

Smile! Relief is here! (This is an imperfect process, remember? Congratulate yourself for reading and "playing" through the book.)

Oh, love me—and right now!—hold me tight! . . . just the way you promised. Now comfort me so I can live, really live; your revelation is the tune I dance to. And let me live whole and holy, soul and body, so I can always walk with my head held high (Ps. 119:76-77,80, *THE MESSAGE*).

Lord, I give myself to You—
my flaws, gifts, passions, dreams and goals.
With You I can hold my head high.

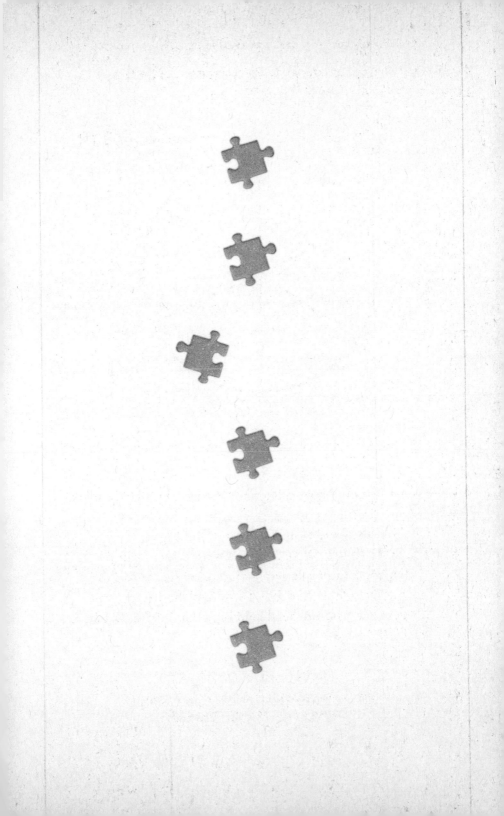

Endnotes

Chapter 1: I Was Perfect Once, but I Didn't Like It Much

1. Dean Paton, "E-serenity, now!" CSMonitor.com, May 10, 2004. http://www.csmonitor.com/2004/0510/p11s02-stct.html (accessed May 2007).
2. Jerry White, *Making Peace with Reality* (Colorado Springs, CO: Navpress Publishing Group, 2002), p. 33.
3. Joanna Weaver, *Having a Mary Heart in a Martha World* (Colorado Springs, CO: Waterbrook Press, 2002), p. 51.
4. Donald McCullough, *The Consolations of Imperfection* (Grand Rapids, MI: Brazos Press, 2004), p. 144.
5. William Collins, *Pocket Webster School and Office Dictionary* (New York: Pocket Books, 1990), c.f. "perfection."
6. Dr. Larry Crabb, *Inside Out* (Colorado Springs, CO: Navpress Publishing Group, 2007), p. 74.
7. Collins, *Pocket Webster School and Office Dictionary*, c.f. "perfectionism."
8. McCullough, *The Consolations of Imperfection*, p. 16.
9. Diane Fassel, *Working Ourselves to Death* (San Francisco: HarperSanFrancisco, 1990), p. 4.
10. Veronica Ray, "I'm Good Enough," *Moment to Reflect* series (Center City, MN: Hazelden Publishing, 1991).

Chapter 2: Doesn't God Want Me to Be Perfect?

1. Kathy Vick, *Lessons in Buoyancy: Letting Go of the Perfect Proverbs 31 Woman* (Grand Rapids, MI: Revell, 2004), p. 13.
2. Enid Howarth and Jan Tras, *The Joy of Imperfection* (Minneapolis, MN: Fairview Press, 1996), p. 5.
3. Mary Pierce, *When Did I Stop Being Barbie and Become Mrs. Potato Head?* (Grand Rapids, MI: Zondervan, 2003), p. 158.
4. Richard Peace, *Learning to Love Ourselves* (Colorado Springs, CO: Navpress Publishing Group, 1994), p. 27.
5. Steve Brown, quoted by Nancy Kennedy in *When Perfect Isn't Enough* (Colorado Springs, CO: Waterbrook Press, 2003), p. 11.

Chapter 3: When Playing God Is No Longer My Best Role

1. Quoted in Gordon S. Jackson, compiler, *Never Scratch a Tiger with a Short Stick* (Colorado Springs, CO: NavPress Publishing Group, 2003), p. 149.
2. Enid Howarth and Jan Tras, *The Joy of Imperfection* (Minneapolis, MN: Fairview Press, 1996), p. 97.
3. Nancy Kennedy, *When Perfect Isn't Enough* (Colorado Springs, CO: Waterbrook Press, 2003), p. 61.
4. A. Bennett, quoted in Jackson, *Never Scratch a Tiger with a Short Stick*, p. 148.
5. Jason A. McGarvey, "The Almost Perfect Definition," Research/Penn State, vol. 17, no. 3 (September 1997). Robert B. Slaney, a counseling psychologist in Penn State's College of Education, explains, "There is a whole range of people who have very different ideas about what perfectionism is." Author Jason A. McGarvey writes, "However, there was, and still is, no generally agreed upon, formal definition of the term."
6. *Driving Miss Daisy*, written by Albert Uhry, directed by Bruce Beresford, Majestic Films International, 1989.

7. Maria Ramirez Basco, *Never Good Enough* (New York: Touchstone, 1999), pp. xi-xii.
8. Ibid., pp. xi-xii.
9. Dr. David A. Seamands, *Healing for Damaged Emotions* (Colorado Springs, CO: Victor Books, 1991), p. 78.
10. Dr. Henry Cloud and Dr. John Townsend, *Boundaries* (Philadelphia, PA: Inspiro/Running Press, miniature ed., 1992), p. 10.
11. Carmen Renee Berry, *When Helping You Is Hurting Me* (New York: Crossroads Publishing, 2003), p. 19.
12. Ibid., p. 20.
13. Sandra D. Wilson, *The World According to Me* (Colorado Springs, CO: Victor Books, 1995), p. 15.
14. Mary Pierce, *Confessions of a Prayer Wimp* (Grand Rapids, MI: Zondervan, 2005), p. 42.
15. Ibid., p. 44.
16. Marsha Crockett, *Dancing in the Desert* (Downers Grove, IL: InterVarsity Press, 2003), p. 34.
17. Carol Travilla and Joan C. Webb, *The Intentional Woman* (Colorado Springs, CO: Navpress Publishing Group, 2002), includes five steps: (1) come as you are today, (2) celebrate your yesterdays, (3) commit it all to God, (4) consider your choices, (5) clarify your next steps.
18. Dr. Les Parrot, PhD, quoted in an interview by Joseph. R. Dunn, PhD, "The Anatomy of Control," *Psychology Online* journal, vol. 1, no. 10 (October 2000).

Relief Guide: What's Wrong with Perfection?
1. Enid Howarth and Jan Tras, *The Joy of Imperfection* (New York: Fairview Press, 1996), p. 97.

Chapter 4: Joy! I Don't Have to Fix It All—Including You!
1. Enid Howarth and Jan Tras, *The Joy of Imperfection* (New York: Fairview Press, 1996), p. 201.
2. Dr. Larry Crabb, *Understanding Who You Are* (Colorado Springs, CO: NavPress Publishing Group, 1997), p. 11.
3. Dr. Henry Cloud and Dr. John Townsend, *Boundaries* (Philadelphia, PA: Inspiro/Running Press, miniature ed., 1992), p. 15.
4. Crabb, *Understanding Who You Are*, pp. 9, 12.
5. Jan Johnson, *Enjoying the Presence of God* (Colorado Springs, CO: Navpress Publishing Group, 1996), p. 134.
6. Pat Springle, *Codependency* (Nashville, TN: W Publishing Group, 1990), pp. 49-58.
7. In order to stay committed to your decision to stay off the relational roller coaster, you may need assistance from a counselor, pastor, life coach, spiritual director or support group.

Chapter 5: Will You Just Lighten Up?
1. Recommended life coaches include Joan C. Webb (joan@joancwebb.com), Kristina Bailey (KB@KristinaBailey.com), Joann Pitteloud (joannjourney@yahoo.com).
2. For more information about life coaching, type "life coach" or "life coaching" into an Internet search engine or visit any of the following websites: www.christiancoaches.com, www.christian-living.com, www.lifecoachtraining.com or www.thecoaches.com.
3. Books such as *Telling Yourself the Truth* (with Marie Chapian, Bloomington, MN: Bethany House, 2000) and *Telling Each Other the Truth* (Bloomington, MN: Bethany House, reprint ed., 2006) by William Backus may help with this.
4. Marjorie Holmes, quoted in Terri Gibbs, ed., *Quiet Places of the Heart in Winter* (Nashville, TN: J. Countryman by Word Publishing, 1997), Week Seven (weekend).

5. The *How Bumpy Is My Ride?* (Wheel of Life) exercise is available on page 29 and the Roles Pinwheel exercise on pages 97 to 104 of *The Intentional Woman* (Colorado Springs, CO: Navpress Publishing Group, 2002).

6. Carol Kent, *Secret Longings of the Heart* (Colorado Springs, CO: Navpress Publishing Group, 2nd ed., 2003), p. 129.

7. Elisabeth Elliot, quoted in Gibbs, ed., *Quiet Places of the Heart in Winter*, Week Eight (weekend).

8. We may need to leave when our lives are in danger. Even Jesus didn't stay where He was treated disrespectfully (see John 8:59)—until, of course, He willingly died in our place on the cross.

9. Elisabeth Elliot, quoted in Gibbs, ed., *Quiet Places of the Heart in Winter*, Week Eight (weekend).

10. Barbara Johnson, quoted in Gibbs, ed., *Quiet Places of the Heart in Winter*, Week Seven (day five).

11. Ken Gire, *Intimate Moments with the Savior* (Grand Rapids, MI: Zondervan, 1989), pp. 5-6.

12. Richard Peace, *Learning to Love Ourselves* (Colorado Springs, CO: Navpress Publishing Group, rev. ed., 1994), p. 37.

Relief Guide: Imperfect Relationships and Families

1. Paul Tournier, *To Understand Each Other* (Louisville, KY: Westminster John Knox Press, 2000), p. 29.

2. Gary Collins, *Christian Coaching* (Colorado Springs, CO: Navpress Publishing Group, 2001), p. 81.

Chapter 6: Never Underestimate the Power of a Nervous Breakdown

1. Enid Howarth and Jan Tras, *The Joy of Imperfection* (Minneapolis, MN: Fairview Press, 1996), pp. 26, 28.

2. Later I learned I had supra-ventricular tachycardia, related to an abnormal electrical impulse in my upper heart. I was probably born with it—it's not life-threatening, but it is sometimes exacerbated by stress.

3. Dr. David A. Seamands, *Healing for Damaged Emotions* (Colorado Springs, CO: Cook Communications, 2004), p. 116.

4. Peter Scazzero with Warren Bird, *The Emotionally Healthy Church* (Grand Rapids, MI: Zondervan, 2003), p. 55.

5. Jennifer Mendelsohn, "Brooke Shields: The truth about new moms and depression," *USAWeekend.com*, September 18, 2005. http://www.usaweekend.com/05_issues/050918/050918brooke_shields.html (accessed June 2007).

6. CPAP stands for Continuous Positive Airway Pressure.

7. Dr. David A. Seamands, *Healing for Damaged Emotions*, pp. 112-113. Psalm 42:5 shows that David suffered from depression, perhaps in part because of his mistreatment by King Saul. Elijah, after his victory over the prophets of Baal, succumbed to despair. In Genesis, we see that Abraham had a comparable emotional encounter. In Jonah 4:3, Jonah admitted he wanted to die. In Matthew 26:38, we read that Jesus felt exceeding pain, "even unto death."

8. Ibid.

9. Gerald G. May, MD, *Addiction and Grace* (New York: HarperSanFrancisco, 1988), p. 169.

10. Paul L. Warner, *Feeling Good About Feeling Bad* (Waco, TX: Word, Inc., 1979), p. 21.

11. "There is a rugged honesty about the life of Jesus—every kind of emotion was so clearly recorded and freely expressed, without any sense of shame [or] guilt or imperfection," writes Dr. Seamands in *Healing for Damaged Emotions* (p. 108).

12. King Solomon, credited with writing most of the Proverbs.

Chapter 7: The Invisible Woman Comes Out of Hiding—Flaws and All

1. Enid Howarth and Jan Tras, *Daily Imperfections* (Minneapolis, MN: Fairview Press, 1998), p. 92.

2. Debra Cooper, *Behind the Broken Image* (ACW Press for Remuda Ranch, 2006), p. 155. Remuda Ranch provides intensive inpatient and residential programs for women and girls suffering from eating disorders and related issues. Their Christian-based programs offer hope and healing to patients of all faiths.

3. Sandy Richardson with Susie Wilsie Govier, *Soul Hunger* (ACW Press for Remuda Ranch, 2006), p. 148.

4. Epel helped conduct research on the scientific link between stress and aging. Quote from The Arizona Republic, "Study links chronic stress, aging," November 30, 2004.

5. Lisa M. Sandin, "I am not my body!" *USAWeekend.com*, March 19, 2006, http://www.usaweekend.com/06_issues/060319/060319this_i_believe.html (accessed June 2007).

6. Grayce Gusmano and C. Soozie Bolte, another excellent counselor, practice at Psychological Counseling Services, LTD in Scottsdale, Arizona. Call (480) 947-5739 for information.

7. "Tragic Schiavo Condiction Reportedly Brought on by Deadly Eating Disorder—NEDA Sheds Crucial Light on Silent Killer," from the National Eating Disorders Associations. http://www.edap.org/p.asp?WebPage_ID=804 (accessed June 2007).

8. People with anorexia starve themselves to dangerously thin levels, at least 15 percent below their appropriate weight. People with bulimia binge uncontrollably on large amounts of food—sometimes thousands of calories at a time—and then purge the calories out of their bodies by vomiting, starving, excessive exercise, laxatives or other methods. People with Eating Disorder Not Otherwise Specified (EDNOS) have some but not all of the symptoms of anorexia or bulimia. This and more information about eating disorders and treatment at Remuda Ranch. http://www.remuda-ranch.com/.

9. Statistics from the National Eating Disorders Association. http://www.edap.org/p.asp?WebPage_ID=320&Profile_ID=41138 (accessed June 2007).

Chapter 8: When a Go-Getter Goes Haywire!

1. Enid Howarth and Jan Tras, *Daily Imperfections* (Minneapolis, MN: Fairview Press, 1998), p. 10.

2. "You really love this, don't you, Joan? You just seem to come alive when you're working." This comment came from the first client I took after my burnout necessitated a sabbatical. As she said it, I felt my stomach tighten. I had tried hard to leave this workaholic lifestyle behind. Any statement or situation that reminded me of my excessive behavior sickened me. It's true, I do get a certain high when rushing, working and finding solutions. I am an adrenaline junkie. Experts say the "busy disease" is both a process and a substance addiction. The chemical is adrenaline. As long as the chemical keeps flowing, we medicate the pain and distress of life. For more about the "busy disease," see time-management expert Dianne Fassel's comments in *Working Ourselves to Death* (New York: HarperSanFrancisco, reprint ed. 1992), pp. 3 and 125.

3. "Saboteur" is a term I use with my coaching clients. We all have an inner Saboteur who tries to convince us to maintain the status quo in our lives. Although the Saboteur may have provided protection in the past, now her messages keep you from moving forward. You can detect the Saboteur's work when you hear yourself respond to change or potential growth with "I don't know . . ." or "But, but, but . . ." or "What if?" or "Oh, but I *should* . . ."

4. Anne Wilson Schaef, *Meditations for Women Who Do Too Much* (New York: Harper & Row, 1990), August 3.
5. More examples of Jesus' saying no are found in Luke 8:26-38 and Mark 5:18-20
6. L. B. Cowman, *Streams in the Desert* (Grand Rapids, MI: Zondervan, rev. ed., 1996), March 26.
7. Marsha Crockett, *Dancing in the Desert* (Downers Grove, IL: InterVarsity Press, 2003), p. 33.
8. Debbie Williams, "The Pros and Cons of Multi-Tasking," *The Organized Times* online. http://www.organizedtimes.com/articles2.html (accessed June 2007).
9. Nancy Kennedy, *When Perfect Isn't Enough* (Colorado Springs, CO: Waterbrook Press, 2003), p. 52.
10. Virginia Anderson, "Healthy Living: Too Much to Do," *Atlanta Journal-Constitution*, Nov. 18, 2003, sec. E, p. 1.
11. "Overload," Dictionary.com. WordNet® 3.0. Princeton University. http://diction ary.reference.com/browse/overload (accessed June 2007).
12. Anderson, "Healthy Living: Too Much to Do."

Chapter 9: When the Going Gets Tough, the Tough Get Burned-Out
1. The company's name was Interiors by Joan Builders Showroom. We partnered with contractors, real estate agents, and architects to work with their clients to design or renovate their homes, residences, offices and model homes. We had a 4,000-square-foot one-stop-shopping center including kitchens, floors, walls, furniture, window treatments and accessories.
2. Diane Fassel, *Working Ourselves to Death* (New York: HarperSanFrancisco, 1990), p. 27.
3. Myron Rush, *Burnout* (Colorado Springs, CO: Victor Books, 1987), p. 13.
4. Ibid., pp. 13-14.
5. Debi Stack, *Martha to the Max* (Chicago, IL: Moody Publishers, 2000), p. 163.
6. A turning point is when something happens that *turns* your life in one direction or another, for better or worse, toward or away from something so that the future is not going to be a continuation of the past. (Note: This definition was adapted and condensed from Tom Paterson, Module 3, "The Turning Points Profile" in *Living the Life You Were Meant to Live* [Nashville, TN: Thomas Nelson Publishers, 1998].)
7. Keri Wyatt Kent, *Breathe* (Grand Rapids, MI: Revell Books, 2005), p. 23.
8. Fassel, *Working Ourselves to Death*, p. 128.

Chapter 10: When Bigger-Better-More Squeezes Out Life
1. Linda Dillow, *Calm My Anxious Heart* (Colorado Springs, CO: Navpress Publishing, 1998), p. 27.
2. Jane Chestnutt, "All in a Woman's Day," *Woman's Day*, April 1, 2003, p. 6.
3. Steve Farrar, *Overcoming Overload* (Sisters, OR: Multnomah Publishing, 2004), cover copy.
4. Dennis J. Dehaan, quoted in Terri Gibbs, ed., *Quiet Places of the Heart in Winter* (Nashville, TN: J. Countryman by Word Publishing, 1997), Week 12 (day two).
5. Richard A. Swenson, MD, *The Overload Syndrome* (Colorado Springs, CO: Navpress Publishing Group, 1999), pp. 13, 23.
6. Richard A. Swenson, MD, *Margin: Restoring Emotional, Physical, Financial, and Time Reserves to Overloaded Lives* (Colorado Springs, CO: Navpress Publishing Group, 2004), p. 149.
7. Kevin A. Miller, *Surviving Information Overload* (Grand Rapids, MI: Zondervan, 2004), p. 15.

Chapter 11: That's Not How It's Supposed to Be

1. I had been hunting actively for a way to know God, flipping and searching through the old family Bible displayed on our coffee table and listening for clues during Sunday School.
2. Leslie Williams, quoted in Terri Gibbs, ed., *Quiet Places of the Heart in Winter* (Nashville, TN: J. Countryman by Word Publishing, 1997), Week 13 (day two).
3. Peter Scazzero and Warren Bird, *The Emotionally Healthy Church* (Grand Rapids, MI: Zondervan, 2003), p. 18.
4. Max Lucado, quoted in Gibbs, ed., *Quiet Places of the Heart in Winter*, Week 13 (day one).
5. George Barna, *Revolution* (Carol Stream, IL: Tyndale House Publishers, 2005), pp. 48-49.
6. Lewis B. Smedes's quote from *Forgive and Forget: Healing the Hurts We Don't Deserve* is taken from *Meditations for Christians Who Try to Be Perfect* by Joan C. Webb (San Francisco: HarperSanFrancisco, 1993), Day 178.
7. Brennan Manning and Jim Hancock, *Posers, Fakers, and Wannabes* (Colorado Springs, CO: Navpress Publishing Group, 2003), p. 21.
8. Unknown, Quoted in Gibbs, ed., *Quiet Places of the Heart in Winter*, Week Eight (day four).
9. Manning and Hancock, *Posers, Fakers, and Wannabes*, p. 22.
10. Lisa Beamer shared these thoughts in an interview while she was touring with her book *Let's Roll*, written with Ken Abraham (Carol Stream, IL: Tyndale House Publishers, 2002.)

Chapter 12: Hey, the Sky's Not the Limit!

1. Enid Howarth and Jan Tras, *Daily Imperfections* (Minneapolis, MN: Fairview Press, 1998), p. 166.
2. As my husband pointed out, the careful planning was indeed worth it—if we had not meticulously prepared, we would have been in dire straits when the unexpected occurred. It reminds me of what author Richard Swenson writes about the concept of *margin*: "Margin is the amount allowed beyond that which is needed. It is something held in reserve for contingencies or unanticipated situations," *Margin* (Colorado Springs, CO: Navpress Publishing Group, 2004), p. 91.
3. Carol Travilla and Joan C. Webb, *The Intentional Woman* (Colorado Springs, CO: Navpress Publishing Group, 2002), includes five steps: (1) Come as you are today, (2) Celebrate your yesterdays, (3) Commit it all to God, (4) Consider your choices, and (5) Clarify your next steps.
4. Answering the question *What is good about my life right now?* helps you determine what is in your personal capital account. Then you have the opportunity to optimize that personal capital. Your response to *What concerns me about my life at the current time?* is an opportunity to identify focus for growth. Your response to *What is lacking in my life right now?* gives you the opportunity to make decisions that fill the void.
5. Sheri Rose Shepherd, *His Princess: Love Letters from Your King* (Sisters, OR: Multnomah Gifts, 2004), p. 86.
6. At this point, we have an opportunity to join God in looking for options. Plan B? Plan C? What is realistic? How can we take personal responsibility to adjust to reality, yet move forward with anticipation and joy?

Chapter 13: No Fair Comparing Sufferings!

1. For more information about Nick Vujicic, visit www.lifewithoutlimbs.org.
2. Larry Crabb, *Shattered Dreams* (Colorado Springs, CO: Waterbrook Press, 2002), p. 4.
3. You can read my "Abraham story" on pages 83 to 84 of *The Intentional Woman* (Colorado Springs, CO: Navpress Publishing Group, 2002).

4. Visit www.intentionalwoman.com for more information about experiencing a Life Plan. Several Intentional Woman presenters are also certified IW Life Planners.

Chapter 14: Numb and Number—When Trying Too Hard Dulls Your Soul

1. Sheri Rose Shepherd, *His Princess: Love Letters from Your King* (Sisters, OR: Multnomah Gifts, 2004), p. 116.
2. Alan Fine, "Everything I Know About Business, I Learned Playing Golf," *Doors and Hardware*, March 2003. http://www.allbusiness.com/fabricated-metal-product-manufacturing/architectural/507460-1.html (accessed June 2007).
3. Jon Leland, "About JOG," The Joy of Golfing. http://thejoyofgolfing.com/about/ (accessed June 2007).
4. Jan Johnson, *Enjoying the Presence of God* (Colorado Springs, CO: Navpress Publishing Group, 1996), p. 18.
5. Shepherd, *His Princess: Love Letters from Your King*, p. 100.
6. Linda Dillow, *Calm My Anxious Heart* (Colorado Springs, CO: Navpress Publishing, 1998), p. 18.
7. Karen Lee-Thorpe, *Waking Up from the Dream of a Lifetime* (Colorado Springs, CO: Navpress Publishing Group, 2005), p. 82.
8. Johnson, *Enjoying the Presence of God*, p. 8.
9. Elizabeth Prentiss, quoted in L. B. Cowman, *Streams in the Desert*, vol. 2 (Grand Rapids, MI: Zondervan, 1966), February 11.

Chapter 15: I Double Dare You!

1. Joan C. Webb, *Devotions for Little Boys and Girls* series (Cincinnati, OH: Standard Publishing, 1992, 1995).
2. Quoted in Pamela Hoover Heim, *Nurturing Intimacy with God* (Nashville, TN: Thomas Nelson Publishers, 1990), p. 153.
3. Ruth Haley Barton, *Sacred Rhythms* (Downers Grove, IL: InterVarsity Press, 2006), p. 24.
4. Oswald Chambers, *My Utmost for His Highest* (Uhrichsville, OH: Barbour Books, new ed. 2006).
5. For inspiration and practical ideas to start your own spiritual journal, read *How to Keep a Spiritual Journal* by Ron Klug (Minneapolis, MN: Augsburg Fortress Publishers, rev. ed., 2002).
6. Jan Johnson, *Enjoying the Presence of God* (Colorado Springs, CO: Navpress Publishing Group, 1996), p. 126.
7. For more information about what fits your temperament, browse the book *Soultypes: Matching Your Personality and Spiritual Path* by Sandra Krebs Hirsch and Jane A. G. Kise, (Minneapolis, MN: Augsburg Fortress Publishers, 2006).
8. Tony Jones, *Read. Think. Pray. Live.* (Colorado Springs, CO: Navpress Publishing Group, 2003), p. 33. I highly recommend this book for its clear, accessible overview of the four parts of the *lectio divina*.
9. My friend's husband eventually decided to follow Christ and they team-taught a Bible class. They've experienced challenges, yet God has made a profound different in their lives. I'm not the only one who prayed for them, but it's my privilege to join with these unknown pray-ers and watch God work.
10. Krebs Hirsch and Kise, *Soultypes: Matching Your Personality and Spiritual Path*.
11. Richard J. Foster, *Prayer: Finding the Heart's True Home* (New York: HarperSanFrancisco, 1992), p. 8.

Relief Guide: Imperfect Faith, Prayer and Spirituality
1. Adapted from an exercise on page 68 of *The Intentional Woman* by Carol Travilla and Joan C. Webb (Colorado Springs, CO: Navpress Publishing Group, 2002).

Chapter 16: Permission to Exhale
1. Another way is to breathe out through your nose instead of your mouth.
2. Rosamunde Pilcher, *Flowers in the Rain and Other Stories* (London: Hodder & Stoughton, Ltd., 1992).
3. Brennan Manning and Jim Hancock, *Posers, Fakers, and Wannabes* (Colorado Springs, CO: Navpress Publishing Group, 2003), p. 22.
4. Carol Kent, *Tame Your Fears* (Colorado Springs, CO: Navpress Publishing Group, reprint ed., 2003), pp. 17-21. Kent calls these forms of fear "slavish fears" (p. 13).
5. "How precious it is, Lord, to realize that you are thinking about me constantly!" (Ps. 139:17-18).
6. "For we are God's masterpiece. He has created us anew in Christ Jesus, so that we can do the good things he planned for us long ago" (Eph. 2:10, *NLT*).

Chapter 17: Trading Exhausting Expectations for Imperfect Joy
1. Sandy Richardson with Susie Wilsie Govier, *Soul Hunger* (ACW Press for Remuda Ranch, 2006), p. 142.
2. Laura Whitworth, Karen Kimsey-House, Henry Kimsey-House, Phil Sandahl, *Co-Active Coaching* (Mountain View, CA: Davies-Black Publishing, 2nd ed., 2007).
3. Carol Travilla and Joan C. Webb, *The Intentional Woman* (Colorado Springs, CO: Navpress Publishing Group, 2002), p. 114.
4. Katie Brazelton, *Pathway to Purpose for Women* (Grand Rapids, MI: Zondervan, 2005), p. 70.
5. Louisa Rogers, "Nurturing Yourself with Self-Esteem," a Care-Note (St. Meinrad, IN: One Caring Place, 1998). I do believe God brought these words to my attention, although I wasn't actively searching for this truth.
6. Liz Curtis Higgs, quoted in Terri Gibbs, ed., *Quiet Places of the Heart in Winter* (Nashville, TN: J. Countryman by Word Publishing, 1997), Week Two (day five).
7. I purchased it at Staples. It's a part of their "That was easy!" branding campaign.
8. To help you discover your personality preferences, take the abbreviated Pace/Priority Assessment tool (based on DISC) in chapter 3 of *The Intentional Woman* (Colorado Springs, CO: Navpress Publishing Group, 2002) or email summit1995@aol.com to purchase the in-depth online tool. To determine your spiritual gift(s), read *Discover Your Spiritual Gifts* (Ventura, CA: Regal Books, 2005) and take the *Finding Your Spiritual Gifts Questionnaire* (Ventura, CA: Gospel Light, 2006), both by C. Peter Wagner. To assess your inherent temperament, take the shortened Kiersey Temperament Sorter II tool (based on the Meyers-Briggs assessment tool) in *Please Understand Me II* by David Kiersey (Del Mar, CA: Prometheus Nemesis Book Co., 1998), pp. 5-11. To discover your unique passions and talents, read *LifeKeys* by Jane Kise and Sandra Krebs Hirsh (Minneapolis, MN: Bethany House, rev. ed., 2005).

Interacting with the Author

Joan C. Webb, a recovering workaholic, perfectionist and burn-out victim, communicates a message of freedom and renewal. In an age of over-choice and over-commitment, she shares refreshing news that God will "guide you always . . . satisfy your needs in a sun-scorched land" and make you like a "well-watered garden, like a spring whose waters never fail" (Isa. 58:11).

Joan is a freelance speaker, trainer and author who has authored or co-authored nine books, including *The Relief of Imperfection, The Intentional Woman* (coauthored with Carol Travilla), *Meditations for Christians Who Try to Be Perfect* and a four-book series titled *Devotions for Little Boys and Girls*. She also wrote study notes for several Old Testament books in Zondervan's *Women of Faith Study Bible*.

As a personal life coach and Intentional Woman Life Plan (IWLP) facilitator, Joan has accumulated hundreds of hours coaching and helping set people free from what holds them back to become who God gifted them to be. Joan's practical and interactive presentations include stories from her background in business, ministry and travel to the Middle East doing relief and development work. Joan and her husband, Richard, live in Chandler, Arizona, and have a daughter, a son and six young grandchildren.

Contacting Joan

- For *Relief of Imperfection* updates, news, facilitator tips and a schedule of Relief of Imperfection retreats,

workshops and presentations, visit www.reliefofim
perfection.com.

· Concerning *The Intentional Woman* five-step process,
visit www.intentionalwoman.com to view information,
updates, facilitator tips and a list of speakers/facilita-
tors in the growing Network of Intentional Woman
Presenters.

· For information about Joan's life-coaching and life-
planning or about her Intentional Writing seminars
and workshops for beginning to intermediate writers,
or to inquire about Joan's speaking, facilitating or
training at your event, visit www.joancwebb.com or
email her at joan@joancwebb.com.

Inspiring Reading for Women

Warrior Chicks
Rising Strong, Beautiful and Confident
Holly Wagner
ISBN 978.08307.44800

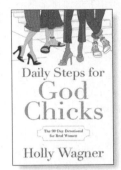

Daily Steps for God Chicks
The 90-Day Devotional for Real Women
Holly Wagner
ISBN 978.08307.39301

When Women Worship
Creating an Atmosphere of Intimacy with God
Amie Dockery with *Mary Alessi*
ISBN 978.08307.42790

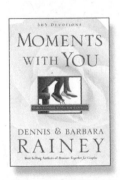

Moments with You
Daily Connections for Couples
Dennis and Barbara Rainey
ISBN 978.08307.43841

The Beauty of Aging
Growing Older with Grace, Gratitude and Grit
Karen O'Connor
ISBN 978.08307.42776

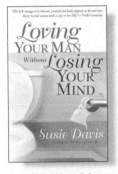

Loving Your Man Without Losing Your Mind
Susie Davis
ISBN 978.08307.43711